Tiger King: Murder, Mayhem and Madness

The third volume in the Docalogue series, this book explores the significance of the documentary series *Tiger King: Murder, Mayhem and Madness* (2020), which became "must-see-TV" for a newly captive audience during the global COVID-19 pandemic.

The series – a true-crime, tabloid spectacle about a murder-for-hire plot within the big cat trade – prompts interesting questions about which documentaries become popular in particular moments and why. However, it also raises important questions related to the medium specificity of documentary in the streaming era, as well as the ethics of both human and animal representation. By combining five distinct perspectives on the Netflix documentary series, this book offers a complex and cumulative discourse about *Tiger King*'s significance in multiple areas, including, but not limited to, animal studies, queer theory, genre studies, labor relations, and digital culture.

Students and scholars of film, media, television, and cultural studies will find this book extremely valuable in understanding the significance of this larger-than-life true-crime documentary series.

Jaimie Baron is Associate Professor of Film Studies at the University of Alberta. She is the author of two books, *The Archive Effect: Found Footage and the Audiovisual Experience of History* (2014) and *Reuse, Misuse, Abuse: The Ethics of Audiovisual Appropriation in the Digital Era* (2020), as well as numerous journal articles and book chapters. She is also the director of the Festival of (In)appropriation, a yearly international festival of short experimental found footage films and videos.

Kristen Fuhs is Associate Professor of Media Studies at Woodbury University. She writes about documentary film, the American criminal justice system, and contemporary celebrity, and her work has appeared in journals such as *Cultural Studies*; the *Historical Journal of Film, Radio, and Television*; and the *Journal of Sport & Social Issues*.

Docalogue

Series Editors: Jaimie Baron and Kristen Fuhs

Each book in the Docalogue book series highlights a recent documentary film from five different scholarly perspectives. By focusing on a single documentary from multiple points of view, each book demonstrates the ways in which a single film can open onto diverse questions having to do with the status of the "real," documentary ethics, and the politics of representation, among other issues. The book series is an extension of Docalogue.com, a monthly online publication that consists of short essays about contemporary documentary films.

I Am Not Your Negro
A Docalogue
Edited by Jaimie Baron and Kristen Fuhs

Kedi
A Docalogue
Edited by Jaimie Baron and Kristen Fuhs

Tiger King: Murder, Mayhem and Madness
A Docalogue
Edited by Jaimie Baron and Kristen Fuhs

For more information on the series, visit: www.routledge.com/Docalogue/book-series/DOCALOGUE

Tiger King: Murder, Mayhem and Madness

A Docalogue

Edited by Jaimie Baron and Kristen Fuhs

Routledge
Taylor & Francis Group

NEW YORK AND LONDON

First published 2022
by Routledge
605 Third Avenue, New York, NY 10158

and by Routledge
2 Park Square, Milton Park, Abingdon, Oxon, OX14 4RN

Routledge is an imprint of the Taylor & Francis Group, an informa business

Library of Congress Cataloging-in-Publication Data
A catalog record for this title has been requested

ISBN: 978-0-367-72182-4 (hbk)
ISBN: 978-0-367-74330-7 (pbk)
ISBN: 978-1-003-15720-5 (ebk)

DOI: 10.4324/9781003157205

Typeset in Times New Roman
by Apex CoVantage, LLC

Contents

Figures

Foreword

Docalogue began in 2017 – and continues – as an online journal, but it also began as a documentary salon in Los Angeles a decade earlier when the editors were both graduate students. Each month, we and a number of friends and colleagues would meet at one of our homes to watch and discuss a documentary film. Although the salon only lasted a year or so, it was one of the most stimulating forums for discussion of documentary film that we experienced during our graduate years. When the editors each moved on to academic jobs in different cities, we continued to meet at conferences, particularly Visible Evidence, which provides a major forum for documentary screening and discussion. Although Visible Evidence is always exciting and generative, we longed to have a way to sustain our discussions of documentary media throughout the year. From this desire arose Docalogue, a digital publication wherein we select one recent documentary each month and solicit two scholars to write a short essay about it, offering two perspectives intended to start off a broader conversation, whether on the website, in classrooms, or within documentary scholarship more broadly.

After about a year of provocative posts in this form, we decided that we might expand the Docalogue format to include short, edited books offering multiple perspectives on a single documentary film – a format that had rarely been tried, at least for nonfiction media. One of the challenges we have faced is how to decide which documentaries to choose as subjects of book-length study. On the website, this is less pressing since we feature so many documentaries, and the purpose is simply to foster scholarly conversation. In choosing documentaries for the book series, however, we are by definition singling out particular documentaries that we think have more than passing significance. And, since our focus is on recent documentaries, this is necessarily a gamble: we do not know for certain which films will stand the test of time. In addition, while our aim is not to establish a new canon, by virtue of focusing a whole book on a film, we cannot help but raise the profile of the film at least within the documentary scholarly community. In the end, we decided to take the risk and simply choose films that we believe raise important issues about documentary in the contemporary moment and open themselves up to multiple avenues of scholarly analysis. Moreover, our aim is also to center at least some films that emerge from makers whose voices have not always been foregrounded by documentary scholarship.

The purpose of the Docalogue book series is, however, not to close the book, as it were, on any film. The idea is to open up conversation among scholars, to demonstrate to students the many ways of approaching a documentary text, and to offer a resource for those who wish to teach recent documentary films about which little has been written so far. We hope that, like the online journal, the book series will give rise to further scholarship about the films in question.

We would like to thank our Board of Advisors – Chris Cagle, Timothy Corrigan, Oliver Gaycken, Maria Pramaggiore, Pooja Rangan, Mila Turajlić, and Janet Walker – for their advice and suggestions regarding the selection of films and writers. Thanks to Natalie Foster, Sheni Kruger, Emma Sherriff, and the whole team at Routledge for supporting this series. A special thanks to Elizabeth Affuso, Luke Pebler, and Suzanne Scott for Angel City talking about *Tiger King*. Finally, our gratitude goes out to all the writers who have contributed thus far to the Docalogue project – both in the book series and on the website.

For more information about the Docalogue, go to www.docalogue.com.

Introduction

The spectacle of *Tiger King*

Kristen Fuhs

On April 8, 2020, less than a month after President Trump declared the COVID-19 pandemic a national emergency, he joined the White House Coronavirus Task Force for their daily press briefing. After a typically meandering opening statement, the president took a few pointed questions from the press corps about the administration's handling of the pandemic before *New York Post* reporter Steven Nelson posed an altogether unrelated question. "Aside from these briefings," Nelson said, fluffing Trump's ego, one of the "biggest ratings hits of the Coronavirus" has been a "show on Netflix called *Tiger King*."[1] He went on to explain that the star of the show, Joe Exotic, claimed he had been unfairly convicted and was seeking a presidential pardon. After a brief back and forth – where it became clear Trump was not one of the purported 34 million people who had watched the documentary series within the first 10 days of its release on March 20 – the president promised to take a look at Joe Exotic's case.[2] On the day of this briefing, there were more than 400,000 confirmed cases of the coronavirus in the United States, more than 10 million Americans were newly out of work, and the death toll in the country approached 15,000. So, despite the series' cultural popularity, the import placed on *Tiger King* as a topic of presidential interest was a bit confounding.[3] As Yohanna Desta sardonically quipped in her *Vanity Fair* piece on this White House *Tiger King* exchange, "That sound you hear is an infinite scream, not least because this ridiculous situation is unfolding against the backdrop of a pandemic."[4]

Flash forward to January 19, 2021, President Trump's final day in office. The question of whether the president would pardon Joe Exotic was once again thrust into the media spotlight when the UK tabloid *Metro* reported that the former zookeeper's legal team was so confident that he'd receive a pardon that they had "a limo parked near his prison – and hair and makeup at the ready."[5] I experienced this story via viral meme the following day, when news circulated that Joe Exotic's hopes for a last-minute pardon had

DOI: 10.4324/9781003157205-1

been dashed. As the image of his mugshot photoshopped onto an idling limousine bounced around my social media feeds, I couldn't help but think it represented a fitting visual to mark a year – and a presidency – that had been characterized by so much denial and loss. The escapades of Joe Exotic, Carole Baskin, and the rest of the big cat trade's merry band of misfits might have captured the public's imagination during the early weeks of the pandemic when it seemed like it might only last a short time. But as President Trump left office, the coronavirus continued to surge, and the US death toll topped 400,000.[6] Meanwhile, our ostensible leader continued to proffer denials of both responsibility and reality, and an ever-increasing partisan divide – around everything from masks, to vaccines, to the integrity of the recent presidential election – was cemented as a defining factor of his presidential legacy. The farce of the Joe Exotic sideshow paled in comparison to the mockery our tabloid president made of governance during this crisis.

The *Metro* story about Joe Exotic, and its subsequent circulation by other media outlets, was a manufactured media event, clearly meant to generate clickbait and thrust Joe Exotic's story back into the public eye almost nine months after the viral popularity of *Tiger King* made him a household name. This moment of tabloid sensationalism was pure media spectacle, from the visual excess of the stretch limousine to the perceived "newsworthiness" of a story about a pop culture figure who was unlikely to have been considered for a pardon in the first place. Four years earlier, and one month into the beginning of Donald Trump's presidential term, historian Robert Zaretsky wrote about "spectacle" for the *New York Times*, suggesting that Guy Debord's *Society of the Spectacle* (1967), more than any other philosophical work of the 20th century, could help us understand the presidency of Donald Trump.[7] He contended that Debord's indictment of a "spectacular society" offered a framework for understanding the mass media's relentless coverage of the rise of Trumpism, as well as our own addiction to consuming the increasingly spectacular stories and images he generated. As every day of Trump's nascent presidency brought "a new scandal, lie or outrage," Zaretsky observed, it became "increasingly difficult to find our epistemological and ethical bearings." He concluded that, when it came to the media's relationship to Trump: "the spectacle swallows us all."

For Debord, spectacle was a concept for making sense of a society "organized around the production and consumption of images, commodities, and staged events."[8] It represented what he saw as a cultural shift where our ties to the natural and social world – the things that were "directly lived" – had "become mere representation" and where the "only thing into which the spectacle plans to develop is itself."[9] Taken that way, spectacle certainly offers a framework for examining Donald Trump's journey from grifter to reality TV star to president to pariah. But spectacle also offers a productive lens for thinking through the immense popularity of *Tiger King* and its cultural impact in a time of global pandemic. As its release coincided with shelter-in-place orders in the United States and around the world, a newly captive audience of Netflix viewers voraciously consumed episodes of the docuseries. Social media engagement around the show exploded as viewers commented on plot twists and turns, celebrities used Twitter to "cast" themselves in future biopics, and users shared memes that irreverently connected the series to the lived experience of lockdown life. For a brief time, during this moment of immense social upheaval, the spectacle of *Tiger King* swallowed us all.

On the one hand, spectacle is built into the visual design of *Tiger King*, and it is an organizing logic for thinking through the series' aesthetic of excess. Across its 318 minutes (seven original episodes, each running between 41 and 49 minutes), the series is oversaturated with plot: murder-for-hire schemes, employee maulings, organized crime, animal rights' feuds, multipartner marriages, runs for political office, civil lawsuits, dead animals, a missing husband, suicide, and more. However, this surfeit of plot – what Pavithra Prasad has called a "numbing abundance of sensationalism" – is overshadowed by the big personalities that populate the docuseries.[10] The people at the heart of this story – Joe Exotic, Carole Baskin, and Doc Antle – are all larger-than-life figures, and spectacle pervades the highly constructed, over-the-top performances of self that were both collected (through archival images) and elicited (for the series itself) by directors Rebecca Chaiklin and Eric Goode. In fact, as Kate Fortmueller discusses in this volume, *Tiger King*'s directors and subjects seem to have at times worked together on aspects of mise-en-scène – costume, hair, makeup, framing, and staging – to reinforce, and in fact exalt, the performative identities at the center of this story.

Spectacle also pervades the framing of the supporting figures in *Tiger King*, as is evident in the overdetermined staging of their various interview tableaux. John Finlay, Joe Exotic's former husband, is unexplainedly shirtless throughout the series. With pierced nipples, missing front teeth, and a lower-abdomen tattoo identifying him (or his genitals?) as Joe Exotic's private property, *Tiger King* frames Finlay as a hillbilly boy toy. A fellow worker at the zoo, Kelci "Saff" Saffery, probably has the most dramatic introduction in the series. Episode 2 opens with a 911 call and footage of the aftermath of his mauling by one of the tigers at G.W. Zoo. With a sort of cool, laid-back resignation, Saff recounts the experience of his resulting amputation amidst the used propane tanks, flat tires, and general detritus that populate the unkempt junkyard in which the filmmakers have staged his interview. As the series goes on, these framings become increasingly baroque. Howard Baskin, Carole's husband, celebrates Joe Exotic's felony conviction for the camera with a split of champagne and a bowl of shrimp cocktail in Episode 7. In the same episode, Allen Glover, G.W. Zoo handyman and putative assassin-for-hire, gives an interview from his bathtub.

Subject framings like these seem designed for shock value, for eliciting a stunned, incredulous reaction from the viewing audience. This is spectacle, via formal arrangement and aesthetic design. But the historical circumstances of *Tiger King*'s release – government mandated stay-at-home orders combined with Netflix's 167 million worldwide subscribers – also created the conditions for a spectacular audience response to the series. As Bruce Magnusson and Zahi Zalloua argue, "What makes an event a spectacle – an image that takes on its own life – has everything to do with the reception of the event."[11] In this era of nichification and fragmented audience tastes, television viewers across demographics flocked to *Tiger King*. With a reported 34 million viewers in its first 10 days and 64 million in its first month, *Tiger King* provided for the kind of collective viewing experience that has become increasingly rare in the era of streaming media.[12] As Hannah Boast and Nicole Seymour discuss further in this volume, *Tiger King* created a sense of simultaneity and immediacy that, given the short window of its popularity, harkened back to the experience of watching live, event television.

This shared viewing experience also translated into audience engagement that extended the series' popularity beyond just TV ratings figures. In the days and weeks following its release, *Tiger King* seemed to be at the center of public conversation. An endless stream of Instagram posts, tweets, and TikTok videos dissected the plot, parodied its central characters, and furthered conspiracy theories. Whether users made mundane observations about mullets or engaged in discursive debates about whether Carole Baskin killed her husband (see Tanya Horeck's chapter in this volume), social media was the central vehicle for connection during this time of newfound social isolation, and *Tiger King* memes emerged as the *lingua franca* of spring 2020.

These memes also helped feed the related media industrial economy that sprouted up in the wake of *Tiger King*'s release, which speaks to the commercial imperatives that position spectacle as "an ideology instrumental to advanced capitalism."[13] Trending memes about the series spawned a corresponding flurry of popular press articles that aggregated these social media reactions, and these stories all competed for clicks and page views.[14] In Hollywood news, actors including Nicholas Cage, Rob Lowe, and Kate McKinnon announced plans to star in competing adaptations of the *Tiger King* story; one of these projects, *Joe Exotic*, is in production at the time of this writing in the summer of 2021.[15] Netflix also capitalized on fans' hunger for more *Tiger King* content by adding a new, eighth episode to the series just three weeks after its initial release. Hosted by comedian Joel McHale, the episode took the form of an "after show" special, a format more often associated with reality television narrative practices than documentary. Hastily produced and filmed on the cheap, the episode engages in follow-up conversations with some of the *Tiger King* participants and probes their reactions to the series, as well as their newfound infamy. It is a fascinating artifact of pandemic production practices, filmed as it was under the limitations of lockdown. McHale jokes about shooting the series from his living room couch, and the episode looks like we've all been invited to hop on a Zoom call with our favorite *Tiger King* personalities (Figure 0.1).

Looking back on it now, it is impossible to separate the experience of *Tiger King* from the moment of its release, coming out as it did during the early stages of the coronavirus pandemic and what would become the final year of Donald Trump's presidency. Because of this, rewatching *Tiger King* in preparation for writing this introduction – with a vaccination under my belt and a new president in the White House – feels a bit uncanny. What relevance does *Tiger King* hold now, outside of the scary, frustrating, and sometimes giddy context of lockdown viewing? *Tiger King: A Docalogue* brings together five distinct perspectives on the series that each engage

Figure 0.1 Responding to *Tiger King*'s popularity, Netflix releases an eighth "after show" episode.

differently with this critical question. Together, these five essays generate a complex and cumulative discourse about *Tiger King*'s significance as a documentary text, a TV trend, a preoccupation of digital culture, and an artifact of a moment in history that we are all still very much coming to terms with.

Taking the viewing context of the pandemic as a starting point, the collection opens with Hannah Boast and Nicole Seymour's essay, "Captive audiences: quarantining with *Tiger King*," which examines *Tiger King*'s popularity as a product of "time." Bringing together scholarship from film and media studies, animal studies, and queer theory to draw out the queer ecological dimensions of *Tiger King*, Boast and Seymour propose *liveness* and *queerness* as intertwined critical frameworks for thinking about the significance of the series. By considering the viewing conditions and drag homages to the program, Boast and Seymour explore how *Tiger King* offered viewers a chance to actively manage their time in the spring of 2020, just as it was beginning to feel so out of control.

Chapter 2, "Netflix's docuseries style: generic chaos and affect in *Tiger King*," approaches the series from a media industries standpoint. In the essay, Jorie Lagerwey and Taylor Nygaard use *Tiger King* as a case study to examine Netflix's house style for docuseries. They suggest that the Netflix house style relies on an extreme generic hybridization, what they call "generic chaos," which privileges affective characterization and viewer reactions over intellectual engagement. As a result, they argue, the Netflix docuseries house style has much closer ties to the production practices of reality television than to those of a feature documentary.

In Chapter 3, "#carolebaskinkilledherhusband: the gender politics of *Tiger King* meme culture," Tanya Horeck takes us outside of the documentary text and examines the social media response to *Tiger King*. Her chapter unpacks the cultural logics of *Tiger King* memes, which she argues both repurpose and amplify the ugly gender tropes that lie at the core of the series' narrative. By creating the affective conditions for a sympathetic response to Joe Exotic and a vilification of Carole Baskin, Horeck suggests, *Tiger King* memes cultivate a networked misogyny that seeped into popular responses and became a central, if problematic, element of the series' popularity.

In Chapter 4, "Labor, celebrity, and the carnivalesque world of *Tiger King*," Kate Fortmueller draws on Mikhail Bakhtin's theories of the carnivalesque to critique private zoos, big cat exhibition, and the labor exploitation that is so much a part of this world. While on the surface, these spaces in *Tiger King* may seem to display a loose, libertarian ethos, Fortmueller argues that these zoos instead operate under systems of control that crystalize the labor conditions and inequities of late capitalism. Rather than looking at the series as an oddity or an escape from the conditions plaguing the

United States at the time of its release, then, she suggests that we would do better to examine the ways that *Tiger King* reflects the norms related to patriarchal American culture and neoliberal economic systems.

Finally, Chapter 5, "I'm in a cage": a historical perspective on *Tiger King*'s animals," rounds out the collection by providing historical and species-specific perspectives on exotic animals in captivity. As Bateman argues, the visual culture of animal display reveals a long history of fraught human–animal relations, showing that the moral and ethical questions raised by the private zoos (and their keepers) in *Tiger King* are nothing new. By turning its focus away from the human characters in the story and toward the big cats they keep in captivity, this essay demonstrates how past tendencies of collecting, displaying, and breeding animals can inform our reading of the docuseries and the world of big cat ownership.

As with the previous works in the Docalogue series, the goal of *Tiger King: A Docalogue* is to demonstrate how a single documentary text can open itself up to a diversity of questions and modes of critical interpretation. Our hope is that this collection will just be the beginning of a productive conversation about the relationship between this documentary's cultural popularity and the historical circumstances of its release. In the opening minutes of the first episode of *Tiger King*, a local newscaster tries to provide some context for the Joe Exotic story: "Long before he was ever indicted. . . . Joe Exotic was someone who makes good TV, makes good news. Even if it's a train wreck, you can't help but look." Likewise, we hope you too won't be able to help but look at the generative, thought-provoking essays in this volume.

Notes

1. U.S. Department of State, "Members of the Coronavirus Task Force Hold a Press Briefing," April 8, 2020, www.youtube.com/watch?v=0oG1l0Zrn48
2. Todd Spangler, " 'Tiger King' Nabbed Over 34 Million U.S. Viewers in First 10 Days, Nielsen Says," *Variety*, April 8, 2020, https://variety.com/2020/digital/news/tiger-king-nielsen-viewership-data-stranger-things-1234573602/
3. Derrick Bryson Taylor, "A Timeline of the Coronavirus Pandemic," *New York Times*, March 17, 2021, www.nytimes.com/article/coronavirus-timeline.html; "Coronavirus Updates from April 8, 2020," *CBS News*, www.cbsnews.com/live-updates/coronavirus-pandemic-covid-19-latest-news-2020-04-08/
4. Yohanna Desta, "Trump Mulls a Joe Exotic Pardon: 'I'll Take a Look'," *Vanity Fair*, April 9, 2020, www.vanityfair.com/hollywood/2020/04/trump-tiger-king-joe-exotic
5. Cydney Yeates, "Joe Exotic Has Limo Waiting Near Prison and Filmed 'Thank You Video to Donald Trump' as He Predicts Presidential Pardon," *Metro*, January 18, 2021, https://metro.co.uk/2021/01/18/joe-exotic-has-limo-waiting-near-prison-ahead-of-trump-pardon-verdict-13924205/

6. Adam Geller and Janie Har, "'Shameful': US Virus Deaths Top 400K as Trump Leaves Office," *Associated Press*, January 19, 2001, https://apnews.com/article/donald-trump-pandemics-public-health-coronavirus-pandemic-f6e976f34a6971c889ca8a4c5e1c0068

7. Robert Zaretsky, "Trump and the 'Society of the Spectacle'," *The New York Times*, February 20, 2017, www.nytimes.com/2017/02/20/opinion/trump-and-the-society-of-the-spectacle.html

8. Douglas Kellner, *Media Spectacle* (London and New York: Routledge, 2003), 2.

9. Guy Debord, *The Society of the Spectacle*, trans. Donald Nicholson-Smith (Brooklyn, NY: Zone Books, 2020), 12, 15.

10. Pavithra Prasad, "The Casual Horror of Boredom in *Tiger King*," *Communication, Culture & Critique* 13 (2020): 573.

11. Bruce Magnusson and Zahi Zalloua, "Introduction: From Events to Spectacles," in *Spectacle*, eds. Magnusson and Zalloua (Seattle, WA: University of Washington Press, 2016), 4.

12. Cynthia Littleton, "Netflix: 'Tiger King' Watched by 64 Million Households, 'Love Is Blind' Grabs 30 Million," *Variety*, April 21, 2020, https://variety.com/2020/tv/news/netflix-tiger-king-love-is-blind-viewing-64-million-1234586272/

13. Marco Briziarelli and Emiliana Armano, "Introduction: From the Notion of Spectacle to Spectacle 2.0: The Dialectic of Capitalist Mediations," in *The Spectacle 2.0: Reading Debord in the Context of Digital Capitalism*, eds. Briziarelli and Armano (London: University of Westminster Press, 2017), 20.

14. See, for example: Ehis Osifo, "Tiger King Dropped on Netflix and Here Are All the Hilarious Tweets About It," *Buzzfeed*, March 24, 2020, www.buzzfeed.com/ehisosifo1/tiger-king-netflix-tweets; Dusty Baxter-Wright, "Tiger King Tiktoks Are a Thing and They're Absolutely Savage," *Cosmopolitan*, April 9, 2020, www.cosmopolitan.com/uk/entertainment/a32091564/tiger-king-tiktoks/

15. Benjamin VanHoose, "See John Cameron Mitchell as Joe Exotic on Set of Upcoming Series About the *Tiger King* Figure," *People*, July 19, 2021, https://people.com/tv/john-cameron-mitchell-on-set-joe-exotic-tiger-king-series/

1 Captive audiences

Quarantining with *Tiger King*

Hannah Boast and Nicole Seymour

Shortly after a deadly virus leapt (possibly) from bats or pangolins to humans in late 2019,[1] much of the quarantined Western world found itself enraptured by the spectacle of another boundary breach: humans handling wild cats in Netflix's series *Tiger King: Murder, Mayhem and Madness*. As the program's full title suggests, directors Rebecca Chaiklin and Eric Goode offered a melodramatic melange of reality TV and true crime, with elements of wildlife programming sprinkled in – thus pushing generic boundaries as well. Within ten days of the program's release on March 20, 2020, 34.3 million households had followed the machinations of flamboyant private zoo owner Joseph Maldonado-Passage or "Joe Exotic," his rivalry with animal sanctuary director Carole Baskin, and a motley crew of supporting characters. Within a month, that number had reached 64 million.[2]

Perhaps it is only appropriate that a program about problematic zoos flourished while a zoonotic disease plagued the world. And indeed, beyond their temporal synchronicity and the human/nonhuman boundary issues they both encapsulate – and even beyond the more obvious link of their common "virality" – the connections between *Tiger King* and the COVID-19 pandemic are surprisingly extensive. For one thing, the experience of lockdown is mirrored in the program's thematization of confinement and incarceration. Netflix observed of their success with *Tiger King* and other programs, "We expect viewing to decline and membership growth to decelerate as home confinement ends."[3] Meanwhile, much of *Tiger King* features live tigers confined in cages, and many of the featured workers at Joe Exotic's zoo are formerly incarcerated people. And near the program's end, an incarcerated and disgraced Joe, perhaps missing the ironic resonance with his earlier activities, compares himself to a wild animal trapped in a cage. There is something disingenuous about a white man decrying his dehumanization by imprisonment, given the racialized nature of mass incarceration and his own anti-Black racism – something that, as we discuss later, the program actively erased. But Joe is not completely wrong to say that there

DOI: 10.4324/9781003157205-2

is something animalizing about being stuck indoors. One commonly used phrase under COVID is "cooped up inside," with "coop" a small enclosure for housing chickens.[4] Even the term "quarantine" is applied to animals as well as humans – as when, for example, celebrities seek to cross international borders with their pets.[5] In sum, while "cooped up" like chickens and "quarantined" like dogs, *Tiger King* viewers faced questions about the ethics of caging animals and, perhaps, humans.

Questions of sexuality, reproduction, and family also surround both *Tiger King* and COVID-19. The ethics of exotic animal breeding is a major topic in the program – and, of course, animal incarceration more broadly is often a matter of regulating reproductive processes, from egg laying and milk producing to births that produce new sources of meat. And we could argue that both *Tiger King* and COVID-19 have prompted critical reflection on the normative human family. That is, the camp queerness of Joe Exotic – whose three-way marriage to two younger men, among other peccadillos, is highlighted in the program – spoke to many viewers whose loss of childcare and sudden family togetherness highlighted the failures of the heterosexual nuclear unit. Mareile Pfannebecker and James A. Smith agree: "During lockdown, the nuclear family – with all its loneliness, repression, and hidden violences – is back with a vengeance. Viewed from within it, the queer interspecies counter-family of Joe Exotic's zoo takes on a surprising utopian bent."[6] Some readers may recall the salacious factoid that (presumably heterosexual) divorces across China spiked after lockdown was lifted, prompting officials to institute a mandatory "cooling-off period."[7] Countless articles and op-eds, too, have revealed how COVID-19 has exacerbated the unequal division of heterosexual household labor, with childcare, cleaning, and, now, homeschooling falling disproportionately to women.[8] *Tiger King* offers a respite from the normative family not only in terms of its queer familial and species dynamics but also in not being "family-friendly" viewing. While animals and, specifically, wildlife programming are often associated with children, the program earned an "MA" or "mature adult" rating for "violence, language, sexual content, drug use, and more." "Is Tiger King OK for Kids? No!" concludes "mommy blog" *Lola Lambchops*.[9]

Teasing out these connections, we approach *Tiger King* as two environmental humanists with expertise in film and media studies, animal studies, and queer theory. We propose *liveness* and *queerness* as two keywords to understand the program's popularity and significance. Liveness unites the contemporary phenomena of documentary broadcasting, streaming services, and social media with the enduring appeal of the older institution of the zoo. Queerness is found in the camp elements of the program and the many drag homages thereto, and in the ways that *Tiger King* disturbs species categories and the institution of the family. Through its engagement with liveness and queerness, the program offers new ways to think about time under COVID-19. Liveness is also present in our own "live" writing of this piece during the first wave of the pandemic in our respective locations of the United Kingdom and Germany in summer 2020. At the time of revising this piece in spring 2021, the pandemic has receded in those countries but intensified in others. Liveness complicates the process of writing in ways that remain visible in the text, notably in our use of the present tense. A future reader encountering this piece after the pandemic has ended may be lucky enough to find our verb tenses out-of-time. But from the 2021 present, when we are just beginning to see how COVID-19 has reshaped our world, and with the threat of new zoonotic diseases in the future, it seems premature to speak of pandemics in the past tense.

Watching on COVID time

As liveness is a function of time (as in the notion of "real-time"), we begin with the strangeness of time under COVID-19. We propose, first, that the virus has forced many people into a rather queer relationship with time: chronos rather than kairos.[10] As literary critic Frank Kermode famously clarified, "chronos is 'passing time' or 'waiting time' and 'kairos is the . . . point in time filled with significance, charged with a meaning derived from its relation to the end.'"[11] We don't know how or when the pandemic will end, and thus, we don't know how to make sense of anything. This sense of warped, and specifically slowed, lockdown time was captured in Twitter jokes, such as, "Experts say we may be as little as two days away from finally leaving the March Age. The next epoch is provisionally being called 'April', and is also expected to last 5–10 million years."[12] Less humorously, many of those infected experience unexpected relapses or extended duration of symptoms known as "long COVID" – thus invoking Alison Kafer's notion of "crip time," or the ways that disability compels a "reorientation to time."[13] For Kafer, "crip time" is the correlative of "queer time;" both involve "departures from 'straight' time" that disrupt the expected ordering of our life courses and the organization of past, present, and future.[14] In this sense, we might say that COVID time is "queer" by virtue of the state of suspension into which it has unexpectedly cast many of our lives.[15]

But binge watching a television series, as so many know, is a perfect way to pass time, if not to make sense of things. Here, we might note that *Tiger King* "began as a feature documentary."[16] We would argue that its ultimate serial nature – along with extra episodes, follow-up specials, planned spinoffs, and homage or parody videos, memes, and other paratexts (some discussed below) – has allowed for an even greater passing of quantifiable time and a sense of unfolding that at least gives shape to our days. Of course, *Tiger King* entered not just any entertainment landscape, but one heretofore defined by content saturation and audience fragmentation; viewing platforms have rapidly proliferated, asynchronous streaming has become the norm, and the era of communal "appointment television" has faded. Lucas Mann has described this scenario in terms of "piece[s] of culture . . . moving past and around us at all times, everything simultaneously here and gone. The act of viewership becomes reaching out for something sturdy . . . grabbing on tight." In such a disorienting and isolating time as a pandemic, such "grabbing on" becomes more important than ever. But perhaps more to the point, Mann explains, "[w]hen new content is endless, access constant, any act of laying claim to what to watch, or read or listen to, becomes a snatch at a moment of slowness . . . which is another way of saying relief."[17] Whether perceived as slowing (a relief from the *typically* relentless pace of life and media) or quickening (a way of *passing* time that seems to have slowed or expanded unbearably under COVID), watching *Tiger King* was a chance to unify or actively manage time that had begun to feel out of control, and uniquely so starting in spring 2020.

What does this have to do with liveness? *Tiger King* created a sense of simultaneity, of a widely shared reality, that is crucial to a sense of liveness – especially when we recall that subjective feelings of community, immediacy, intimacy, and intense engagement typically define ("real") live experiences.[18] That is, given the compact and concentrated window of its popularity, this streaming program came about as close as you can get to a traditional network television broadcast (prerecorded, but available to widespread audiences at the same time) if not a simulcast (performed live, but available to widespread audiences at the same time). Further, as a *documentary* series, *Tiger King* offered us "real life" as a subject.[19] Finally, as we explain in more depth later, *Tiger King*'s aura of liveness is inseparable from the pervasive association of wild animals with liveness. That is, the appeal of viewing animals has always been about their "liveness" – their unpredictability, whether a matter of risk and danger or, alternately, charm and humor.[20] Indeed, we could link *Tiger King* to one of television's earliest successes: the live broadcast of *Zoo Parade* that started in 1950 from Chicago's Lincoln Park Zoo; by 1952, when one-third of American homes had televisions, 11 million people were tuning in on Sunday afternoons.[21] In a period of stalled time marked by mass death and anxieties over mortality, these three senses of liveness offered by *Tiger King* (simultaneity, documentary, and animality) proved irresistible.

Here, we are suggesting that "liveness" might be understood as an affective, and not necessarily quantitative, category. We follow the original skeptic of the "live"/"recorded" binary, Philip Auslander, who argued in 2008 that "the concept of liveness describes a historical, rather than ontological condition," one "whose meaning changes over time and is keyed to technological development;" later, he concluded that "it may be that we are now at a point in history at which liveness can no longer be defined in terms of . . . the presence of living . . . beings."[22] We will sketch out this idea further by turning now to the emergent phenomenon of "digital drag," which has likewise flourished in the COVID-19 media landscape and, not incidentally, offered many campy take-offs of *Tiger King*'s protagonists. During a time when drag performers have been losing income from their usual live performances, and when many queer people (such as our students) have had to return to the normative family fold, this phenomenon has offered great relief. While at first our turn to digital drag might seem like a detour, we believe it is justified given how heavily contemporary media phenomena such as *Tiger King* rely upon "paratextual discourse" for their success.[23]

Tiger King and the drag queens

The most prominent project in this vein is drag queen Biqtch Puddin's "Digital Drag Show," which premiered the same day as *Tiger King* on the gaming platform Twitch and featured a mix of live and prerecorded performances. Having become a gleeful devotee of this show, Nicole can speak to the fact that even prerecorded performances carry an exciting sense of liveness due to at least four factors: Biqtch's live hosting and introductions; the chyrons for each performer that list their Venmo, PayPal, or other financial account so that viewers may tip them while watching; the timeliness of many performances (in addition to nods to *Tiger King*, the show acknowledged and fundraised for contemporary causes such as Black Lives Matter protests);[24] related social media aspects such as Twitch's live chat function; and, in Nicole's experience, texting with friends while watching performances.[25] Even when watching archived episodes later (they remain online for a few days before disappearing), that aura of liveness, to riff on Water Benjamin, still inheres. Again, this feeling of liveness was important in the face of mass death, and in terms of creating a pleasurable, playful sense of connection with friends and strangers in a time of disconnection and isolation.

One relevant performance featured on the Digital Drag Show was that of Glasgow, Scotland-based drag artist Rujazzle (Figure 1.1).[26] Over a gleefully chaotic 5 minutes and 55 seconds on the April 17, 2020 show, Rujazzle performed as both Carole Baskin and Joe Exotic, lip-syncing songs including Survivor's "Eye of the Tiger" (of course), Kelis's "Caught

Figure 1.1 Drag artist Rujazzle dazzles as "Joe Exotic" in 2020.
Source: Photo courtesy of Rujazzle.

Out There," and "What Is This Feeling?" from the musical *Wicked*, as well as original dialogue from *Tiger King* and other internet parodies thereof.[27] The Kelis and *Wicked* songs, with their respective choruses of "I hate you so much right now!" and "Loathing, unadulterated loathing," speak humorously to the Joe-Carole rivalry. While performing the latter song, Rujazzle used a mostly seamless-looking split screen to appear simultaneously as both people. This visual technique perhaps allows us to reflect on the simultaneity of the world's embrace of the *Tiger King* phenomenon while adding another level to the typical gender bending of drag performance.

Scholars have explained how the meme, just like drag performance, "live[s] off . . . [the] possibilities of remix and alteration."[28] *Tiger King*, with its colorful characters, memorable one-liners, and mashup of genres, provided the perfect jumping-off point for memeability, drag, and virality to come together. Relatedly, we should consider the ephemerality of digital drag homages to the program. On April 4, 2020, US drag queen Mimi Imfurst hosted an entire *Tiger King*-themed "online drag show" on Facebook Live, for which she promised to "serv[e] Carole Baskin realness."[29] Both of us sadly missed this event, as the URL now explains that "[t]he link you followed may have expired." The "liveness" of drag takes on *Tiger King*, and of the program itself, seems to have a particular shelf life. If we

apply performance theorist Peggy Phelan's work in a perhaps counterin-
tuitive direction, we see again the liveness of *Tiger King*; as Phelan argues
that ephemerality is what defines live performance,[30] then the ephemerality of a viral sensation – or perhaps more precisely, the *expectation* of its
ephemerality – necessarily gives it a certain sense of liveness, as well as
a potential sense of queerness. As scholars such as Jack Halberstam have
shown, ephemerality has often been seen as a queer quality, given how
LGBTQ+ lives have not necessarily been structured for longevity, in light
of everything from biological familial rejection to the AIDS crisis to the
statistical rarity of same-sex parenthood.[31]

We almost suspect that *Tiger King*'s very title was designed to invite
drag responses; another drag queen who has appeared as both Joe and
Carole, the UK's Cheryl Hole, quipped in a related Instagram video,
"Who really is the Tiger King – or Queen??"[32] But even if it were titled
differently, *Tiger King* is so deeply imbued with queer flamboyance and
what Susan Sontag called "pure" or "genuine Camp" – a "mixture of
the exaggerated, the fantastic, the passionate, and the naive" – that its
deliberately campy, semi-mocking embrace by drag performers seems
inevitable.[33] After all, this is a program in which the (anti-)hero sports a
bleached-blonde mullet, wears eyeliner and an eyebrow ring, once ran for
President of the United States, and launched a music "career" during
which he lip-synced to someone else's prerecorded vocals – not unlike
a drag queen. As for Carole, it was not hard for Joe to skewer her by
hiring a look-alike for his music video titled "Here Kitty Kitty," given
her signature penchant for flower crowns and animal print everything;
likewise, it has not been hard for drag queens to act as her look-alikes in
turn. And we haven't even mentioned the melodramatic facts, tailor-made
for campy drag take-offs, that Joe tried to have Carole murdered while
also accusing her of murdering her first husband. Of course, the culture of
camp that has arisen around *Tiger King* is not limited to drag; it includes
everything from TikTok commentary and parodies to a mini-Broadway
musical.[34] Put succinctly, *Tiger King* entered a particular media landscape
already marked by "the mainstreaming of drag performance *and* a wider
investment in camp humour and celebrity culture."[35]

The drag/camp embrace of *Tiger King*'s aesthetics – the "obsess[ion]
with the fashions" that Cheryl Hole's video articulates – necessitates a con-
sideration of the specific aesthetics of the tiger itself. One important source
is the representational legacy of British imperialism in India. British colo-
nizers saw the tiger as a particularly cruel and ferocious animal, imagined
alternately as majestic and as vermin.[36] The tiger has similarly served as
a "metaphor of insurrection," from imperial accounts of the 1857 Indian
Rebellion against British rule to the anti-colonial iconography of the Tamil

Tigers.[37] This history has shaped the common perception of tigers as duplic-itous and cunning – which, we might note, is also a rather queer marking. Indeed, one of the most famous tigers in popular culture, Shere Khan from Disney's *The Jungle Book* (1967), inaugurated the trend of the "mincing, sibilant, underhanded . . . gay villai[n]" in animated film.[38] The tiger, then, holds ambivalent associations with power, sexuality, and subversion that shape its meaning in *Tiger King* and in drag responses.

Joe Exotic's name takes on particular valence in this light. A twist on the "Average Joe" (the title of the first episode being, in fact, "Not Your Average Joe), "Joe Exotic" combines white trash aesthetics with the implication of exotic animals and "exotic dancers" aka strippers – yet another kind of illicit sexuality.[39] Relatedly, tiger skin serves as "erotic shorthand for sex, pleasure and desire" and for "female sexual agency."[40] Josephine Baker, Kim Novak, and countless other sultry starlets of the past have posed on tiger pelts, evoking the tiger's association with "Orien-tal" sensuality and luxury. Similarly, the animal print clothing that Carole so favors, layering multiple different prints at once, is associated with female youth and sexuality, as reflected in the presumed consumer anxiety behind fashion advice on "how to wear animal print . . . and look classy!" "at any age!"[41] These associations set up *Tiger King* for its drag appropria-tions; the program and its reception, we argue, would not work the same way with any other animal.

Zoo time

The popularity of *Tiger King* is inextricable from the broader cultural meanings of the zoo, an institution that similarly bears concerns with live-ness and time, queerness, and the family. Zoos are a major North Ameri-can entertainment experience, alongside movie theaters, theme parks, and football games, with the Association of Zoos and Aquariums (AZA) reporting that its member institutions in the United States receive over 183 million visits per year.[42] AZA-accredited zoos make up only 10% of North American zoos, partly because accreditation requires higher welfare standards.[43] There are thus many more visits to American zoos than are captured in AZA statistics, including visits to Joe's Greater Wynnewood Exotic Animal Park, which, unsurprisingly, is not accredited. Like all the genres that *Tiger King* brings together – reality television, true crime, and wildlife programming, as well as drag responses – the appeal of zoos is founded on liveness. Zoos offer a site of ideally instantaneous encounter with live, "wild" creatures, particularly "charismatic megafauna," includ-ing elephants, gorillas, and, of course, tigers.[44] In modern zoos, the live-ness of animals is typically conscripted into conservation messaging, with the live encounter "disciplining" the zoogoer into an appropriate attitude toward nature.[45] In the case of tigers, the figures indicating the need for conservation are stark: classified as an endangered species, with three species already extinct, only 3,500 tigers remain in the wild.[46] Tigers are quite literally running out of time.

And indeed, zoos often frame their conservation efforts as "buying time" for wild animals,[47] or in relation to a "ticking clock" to which we must attend in order to avert future extinctions.[48] We might therefore understand the zoo more broadly as an institution for managing time. As such, it is a curiously appropriate setting for a documentary series collectively consumed during the fragmented time of lockdown. Day-to-day life in the zoo involves the strict regulation of animal time, in which animals suffer both an excess and lack of time.[49] For example, Joe Exotic's tigers often seem extremely bored, lacking not just space but agency over how they spend their time. These tigers endure an endless expanse of time before them, yet in other ways, their life cycles are heavily circumscribed by breeding programs and the premature endings of their lives when they age out of cuteness and are deemed no longer valuable. (Joe was convicted of, among other things, shooting and killing five tigers, in violation of the Endangered Species Act.) The regulation of nonhuman time in the park is further premised on the control of the time of factory-farmed animals; we see workers unloading expired supermarket meat for the tigers (and themselves) and hacking up a feedlot cow rejected for human consumption to become tiger food. A concern with time is also built into the structure of the program, which begins in media res with Exotic "doing time" in the Grady County Jail.[50] Structured around the parallel experiences of animal and human incarceration, *Tiger King* reminds viewers of their own unwanted, indeterminate confinement and of the expansions and contractions of COVID-19 time.

The management of time in the zoo is also a management of sexuality, one which serves to naturalize heteronormative models of nonhuman and human life. Greater Wynnewood Exotic Animal Park sits in curious relation to this role, both reinscribing it and subverting it, as we discuss later. The connection between zoo time and sexuality occurs in conservation rhetoric, with zoogoers called upon to preserve endangered species so that their future children will be able to see them. This is a version of the "heterosexist, pro-reproductive rhetoric" that Nicole, drawing on Lee Edelman's notion of "reproductive futurism," has identified as a familiar environmentalist trope.[51] Even the most "ethical" zoo is oriented toward a heteronormative future via the "baby" animals it must produce in order to justify its purported conservation goals and, more pertinently, to attract visitors.

Figure 1.2 Cuddling up to wild cubs in *Tiger King* (Rebecca Chaiklin and Eric Goode, 2020).

At Greater Wynnewood Exotic Animal Park and in its travelling exhibitions, tiger cubs are the primary draw. Available to be bottle-fed, petted, and posed with in scenes that violate the prohibition in AZA-accredited zoos against almost all physical contact between visitors and animals, the cubs allow visitors to participate in a distorted vision of cross-species parenting and, in particular, of mothering, through which humans can both coo over and dominate a temporarily diminished fearsome beast (Figure 1.2).[52] Also significant is the fact that the visitors to Greater Wynnewood Exotic Animal Park shown on screen are typically in family groups, mirroring the wider demographics of zoogoing. The AZA states that 69% of visitors to its zoos annually are parties with children, quantifying the benefits of these visits in terms of children's and family experiences.[53] The reputation of the zoo as a locus for "quality family time" to be recorded for the future in family photographs and videos strengthens its potency in activating heteronormative environmental sentiments.[54]

Joe Exotic's zoo relies on these "family-friendly" associations for its income and reinforces standard heteronormative zoo models of animal and human life through its breeding programs. Still, his zoo is an inappropriately "adult" space, seen most evidently in gift shop merchandise that includes Joe Exotic–branded condoms, thong underwear, and lubricant gel instead of animal toys, keyrings, and pencils. Exotic seems congenitally inappropriate, flouting norms of queer respectability through his flamboyant appearance, triple marriage, and love of tigers, with their associations with glamour, drama, and risk. His obsession with animals seems somewhat queer in its suggestion of arrested development or temporal "interruption,"[55] given the persistent marketing of zoos and animals as an interest of children. This refusal of normative temporalities is further seen in Exotic's position as the head of a "queer family" of zoo workers. The workers appear to enact what Harlan Weaver describes as "intimacy without relatedness" or "queer kinship" through their common care for the tigers who sit, like them, at the margins of society, and with whom they rather touchingly share their expired meat.[56] It is worth noting that this community was far from ideal; we ultimately learn of Joe's poor treatment of his workers and partners, while the tigers are held captive in squalid conditions. Nevertheless, even in these failures, *Tiger King* offers a glimpse of an alternative mode of familial relations to those that feel so oppressive to many in the pandemic present.

Tiger King's ambivalent queer potentialities manifest not only in their orientation to its subject matter – the heteronormative institutions of the zoo and the family – but also in terms of genre. One of the documentary genres in which we situate *Tiger King* is wildlife programming, which mirrors the tendency of zoos to affirm the naturalness of heterosexual, nuclear families, and normative life trajectories.[57] The "classical" wildlife documentary, as Cynthia Chris notes, has "frequently contextualized animal behaviors in narratives that allegorize them as lessons in [heteronormative] sex roles and parenting" and "typically features an individual, anthropomorphized animal protagonist, and is often constructed as a 'coming of age story.'"[58] Wildlife documentaries serve to consolidate the family unit through a shared experience of viewing content seen as morally improving in its apparent educational value, serious tone, and prompting of "higher" emotions such as awe through a depiction of "elevating" moments of animal life.[59] The scheduling of the wildlife documentary, typically found in the United Kingdom in the "family-friendly" viewing slot of the evening hours before the 9 pm watershed,[60] has allowed it to play a related role to the zoo as "quality family time." *Tiger King* is likely to recall for many viewers the animal and wildlife programming that has been a regular feature on our televisions since *Zoo Parade* in the 1950s. As with its engagement with the institution of the zoo, *Tiger King* draws its appeal from both adhering to the conservative norms of the wildlife documentary genre and challenging them.

In its reminder of these different family activities, *Tiger King* activates a form of nostalgia that increases the program's appeal by allowing the viewer to recall an earlier, perhaps simpler time. Its adult audiences may be prompted to recall family viewing practices in childhood, a reminder that may have a melancholy inflection, since, while many families were forced together during the pandemic, others were forcibly kept apart, with the young and early adults most likely to have Netflix subscriptions often isolating in shared, rented homes.[61] Equally, by violating the norms of the wildlife documentary, *Tiger King* offers illicit thrills. It punctures the genre's pomposity, yet also, more troublingly, offers an opportunity for "slumming it" by voyeuristically observing the lives of Exotic and his associates.[62] Some might argue, particularly on the basis of the latter, that *Tiger King* is not wildlife programming or documentary programming at all but rather reality TV. Susan Murray has noted "the belief that documentaries should be educational and informative, authentic, socially engaged, independently produced, and serve the public interest, while reality TV programs are commercial, sensational, popular, entertaining, and potentially exploitative and/ or manipulative."[63] We would therefore describe *Tiger King* as an example of what Nicole has called "low environmental" – though not necessarily environmentalist – "culture."[64] That is, it raises questions about serious topics such as animal incarceration and extinction while maintaining none of the "classy" affect of most works that tackle those topics. In doing so, *Tiger King* joins a growing canon of environmental works that trouble the boundaries of genre.

Tiger King's afterlives

Reality television is infamous for its deceptive and manipulative editing. Even so, the decision of directors Chaiklin and Goode to excise Joe's anti-Black racism is suspect given the program's core themes of incarceration and captive time.[65] As activists and scholars have shown, the US criminal justice system functions as a racialized instrument of social control, with mass incarceration – a phenomenon that disproportionately affects young Black men – serving "to define the meaning and significance of race in America."[66] The elision of Joe's racist views in a program structured around his incarceration is curious, to say the least. (It also seems curious given the exoticized and racialized connotations of the tiger.) The program's failure in this regard became starkly apparent immediately after its release in spring 2020, as worldwide Black Lives Matter protests unfolded and the disproportionate impact of COVID-19 on BIPOC communities came to light. We might further understand Joe's abjection and control of animals and his racism as intertwined, premised on an exclusion of both animals and Black people from the category of the "human" and therefore beyond the limits of moral considerability.[67] Perhaps, *Tiger King's* creators thought the program needed an implicit fantasy of racial harmony to function as a collective experience in the way that it did. Nevertheless, for a program to tackle the breaching of human/nonhuman boundaries at this moment *without* addressing race feels disingenuous and reminds us again not to idealize the queer potential of *Tiger King.*

As a piece of trashy pop culture that is now permanently tied to its moment of release during the COVID-19 pandemic, *Tiger King* might seem like a show that would date quickly and soon be forgotten. Nevertheless, this seemingly ephemeral program continues to extend its temporality through various afterlives. In at least one instance, the paratextual drag culture discussed previously extended the shelf life of the program: "You might have thought the *Tiger King* craze was over," observed Kristy Puchko, but on July 1, 2020, drag queens Trixie Mattel and Katya released an episode of their popular Web series *I Like to Watch* centered on it.[68] Meanwhile, at the time of writing, Carole Baskin has just started a stint on *Dancing with the Stars* and fictional adaptations of *Tiger King* starring comedians and camp figures such as Nicolas Cage and Kate McKinnon are currently in the works.[69] The program also briefly revived the fortunes of Joe's zoo, renamed "Tiger King Park" by his former business partner Jeff Lowe and visited by flocks of tourists after Oklahoma lifted its stay-at-home restrictions in May 2020, although it has since been reported as closed for good.[70] A recent viral Tweet reminds us, alongside a wry comment on the winter holidays and commercialization, that the queer pandemic temporalities we have described are far from over: "Can't believe it's nearly lockdown again already. Swear it gets earlier and earlier every year. I walked past a house . . . and [the inhabitant] was already watching tiger king."[71] In fact, both of us, writing in London and Munich, respectively, are anticipating a new set of lockdowns. And of course, this Tweet reminds us that the virus is still very much with us. However unfashionable *Tiger King* might be by the time this essay appears in print, the program and its reception offer unlikely insights into the temporalities and ecologies of pandemics, and a glimpse – even if a flawed one – of the queer kinships that many of us found ourselves craving from the confines of the locked-down family home.

Notes

1. Thom van Dooren, "Pangolins and Pandemics: The Real Source of This Crisis Is Human, Not Animal," *New Matilda*, March 22, 2020, https:// newmatilda.com/2020/03/22/pangolins-and-pandemics-the-real-source-of-this-crisis-is-human-not-animal/
2. Dan Zinski, "Tiger King Is One of Netflix's Most-Viewed Original Shows Ever," *ScreenRant*, April 8, 2020, https://screenrant.com/tiger-king-netflix-viewers-data-ratings-popularity/#:~:text=Only%20Stranger%20Things%20

season%203%2C%20which%20drew%2036.3%20milion%20viewers, for%20Stranger%20Things%20season%203; Dominic Patten, "Netflix Reveals Strong Viewership Numbers for Mindy Kaling's 'Never Have I Ever' & Spike Lee's 'Da 5 Bloods' in Earnings Report," *Deadline*, July 1, 2020, https://deadline.com/2020/07/netflix-viewership-results-mindy-kaling-never-have-i-ever-steve-carell-space-force-spike-lee-da-5-bloods-earnings-report-q2–1202987697/

3. Justin Harp, "Netflix Reveals Tiger King Is One of Its Most-Watched Shows Ever as It Releases Viewing Figures," *Digital Spy*, April 21, 2020, www.digitalspy.com/tv/ustv/a32227946/netflix-tiger-king-viewing-figures/

4. The Oxford English Dictionary describes a "coop" as "[a] kind of basket placed over fowls when sitting or being fattened; a cage or pen of basketwork or the like for confining poultry, etc." "coop, n. 1," *OED Online*, September 2020, Oxford University Press, www.oed.com/view/Entry/41020?rskey=RdaNBU&result=1.

5. "Johnny Depp's Wife Charged With Illegally Bringing Dogs Pistol and Boo Into Australia," *NBC News*, July 16, 2015, www.nbcnews.com/news/world/johnny-depps-wife-charged-illegally-bringing-dogs-pistol-boo-australia-n39294

6. Mareile Pfannebecker and James A. Smith, "Tiger King, COVID-19, and the Nature of Work," *Ceasefire*, May 20, 2020, https://ceasefiremagazine.co.uk/tiger-king-covid-19-and-the-nature-of-work/

7. Lily Kuo and Agencies, "Anger in China at Law Ordering 'Cooling-Off Period' Before Divorce," *The Guardian*, May 29, 2020, www.theguardian.com/world/2020/may/29/anger-in-china-at-law-ordering-cooling-off-period-before-divorce

8. Alexandra Villarreal, "Coronavirus Pandemic Exacerbates Inequalities for Women, UN Warns," *The Guardian*, April 11, 2020, www.theguardian.com/world/2020/apr/11/un-coronavirus-pandemic-gender-inequalities-women

9. "Is Tiger King OK for Kids? No! Here's Why," *Lola Lambchops*, April 4, 2020, https://lolalambchops.com/is-tiger-king-on-netflix-family-friendly/

10. Queer narratologists have discussed the implications of subverting normative time. See, for example, Robyn Warhol and Susan S. Lanser's *Narrative Theory Unbound: Queer and Feminist Interventions* (Columbus, OH: Ohio State University Press, 2015).

11. As quoted in Adeline Johns-Putra, *Climate Change and the Contemporary Novel* (Cambridge, UK: Cambridge University Press, 2019), 165.

12. As quoted in Diletta De Cristofaro, "'Every Day Is Like Sunday': Reading the Time of Lockdown via Douglas Coupland," *b20*, May 13, 2020, www.boundary2.org/2020/05/diletta-de-cristofaro-every-day-is-like-sunday-reading-the-time-of-lockdown-via-douglas-coupland/

13. Alison Kafer, *Feminist, Queer, Crip* (Bloomington, IN: Indiana University Press, 2013), 27.

14. Ibid., 34.

15. For other insightful perspectives on this phenomenon, see the co-authored academic blog "Times of COVID-19," *Times of COVID-19*, 2020, https://timesofcovid19.temporalities.no/. Thanks to Hugo Reinert for drawing it to our attention.

16. Steve Greene, "'Tiger King': How Two Directors Untangled the Thorny Web Around Big Cat Owners," *IndieWire*, March 24, 2020, www.indiewire.com/2020/03/tiger-king-directors-netflix-interview-1202220039/

17. Lucas Mann, "How to Miss What Isn't Gone: Thoughts on Modern Nostalgias While Watching 'The Office,'" *Los Angeles Review of Books*, May 24, 2020, https://lareviewofbooks.org/article/how-to-miss-what-isnt-gone/

18. See Daniel Meyer-Dinkgräfe, "Liveness: Phelan, Auslander, and After," *Journal of Dramatic Theory and Criticism* 29, no. 2 (2015): 70, 72–3, drawing on Bundy et al. and Reason and Barker. *Tiger King* was the most-Tweeted-about TV show from March 20 to 29, with 1.8 million related interactions. Todd Spangler, "'Tiger King' Nabbed Over 34 Million U.S. Viewers in First 10 Days, Nielsen Says (EXCLUSIVE)," *Variety*, April 8, 2020, https://variety.com/2020/digital/news/tiger-king-nielsen-viewership-data-stranger-things-1234573602/

19. The other must-see television show during this period was also a documentary series, the Michael Jordan-focused *The Last Dance* (Jason Hehir, 2020).

20. Live animals more generally have proven quite a draw during COVID-19, with many locked-down audiences seeking out animal encounters via "nestcams" and live feeds from animal sanctuaries that, in contrast to *Tiger King*, offer a sense of life continuing as normal. See Jonathan Turnbull, Adam Seale, and William M. Adams, "Quarantine Encounters With Digital Animals: More-Than-Human Geographies of Lockdown Life," *Journal of Environmental Media* 1, no. 1 (2020).

21. Gregg Mitman, *Reel Nature: America's Romance with Wildlife on Film*, second edition (Seattle, WA: University of Washington Press, 2012), 133.

22. Philip Auslander, *Liveness: Performance in a Mediatized Culture*, second edition (New York: Routledge, 2008), XII; Philip Auslander, "Digital Liveness: A Historico-Philosophical Perspective," *PAJ: A Journal of Performance and Art* 34, no. 3 (2012).

23. John Mercer and Charlie Sarson, "Fifteen Seconds of Fame: Rupaul's Drag Race, Camp, and 'Memeability'," *Celebrity Studies* (2020): 11.

24. Digital Drag Show supporters raised $16,000 in the latter's honor for civil rights organization Color of Change.

25. It's worth noting here that John Mercer and Charlie Sarson explain that social media is the way that drag queens have to build their profile: "Having neither the financial resources nor the social and cultural capital of [Hollywood A list] stars, [drag queens] are often their own publicity machine and sustain their celebrity statuses online through Instagram, Twitter, and associated social media." Mercer and Sarson, "Fifteen Seconds," 9.

26. Rujazzle, "TIGER KING . . . by a Drag Queen! RUJAZZLE," YouTube, April 18, 2020, video, 5:55, https://youtu.be/Jh4xlHi6iBA

27. This lip-syncing of dialogue may remind some of the TikTok videos of comedian Sarah Cooper mouthing audio of Donald Trump – which went viral just a week later.

28. Paasonen, Jarrett, and Light, as quoted in Mercer and Sarson, "Fifteen Seconds," 6.

29. Mimi Imfurst (@MimiImfurst), "Tiger King Online Drag Show – I Will He Serving Carole Baskin Realness Sat Rsvp Here www.facebook.com/events/1340899392765910," *Twitter*, April 1, 2020, https://twitter.com/mimiimfurst/status/1245402160025808897?lang=en. "Realness" is a turn of phrase from drag culture that refers to the "flawless execution of a particular impression or performance." Gary Hartley, "A Beginner's Guide to Drag Terminology," *Cape Town Magazine*, n.d., www.capetownmagazine.com/arts-culture/a-beginners-guide-to-drag-terminology/104_22_19320

30. Peggy Phelan, *Unmarked: The Politics of Performance* (New York: Routledge, 1993), 31, 146.
31. Jack Halberstam, *In a Queer Time and Place: Transgender Bodies, Subcultural Lives* (New York: New York University Press, 2005), 2.
32. Similarly, the version of Rujazzle's performance now posted on YouTube promises in its title, "TIGER KING . . . by a Drag Queen!"
33. Susan Sontag, "Notes on 'Camp,'" *Partisan Review* 31, no. 4 (1965): 6, 7.
34. Broadway.com, "Kristin Chenoweth – 'Little Pieces' – TIGER KING: THE MUSICAL (A Parody!) – (Official Video)," YouTube, April 15, 2020, video, 4:37, https://youtu.be/bAQau6pJpPA
35. Mercer and Sarson, "Fifteen Seconds," 3, our emphasis. Esther Newton's 1978 preface to her foundational work on drag, *Mother Camp: Female Impersonators in America*, predicted this turn: "[T]he gay sensibility, like that of other minorities before it, is finding, in watered down form, a larger audience" (XII).
36. John Miller, *Empire and the Animal Body: Violence, Identity and Ecology in Victorian Adventure Fiction* (London: Anthem Press, 2012), 37. Both meanings conveniently justified the tiger's elimination, whether as demonstration of imperial might or as "care" toward India's colonized population. Miller, *Empire and the Animal Body*, 37–8.
37. Miller, *Empire and the Animal Body*, 40; John Miller, "Rebellious Tigers, a Patriotic Elephant and an Urdu-Speaking Cockatoo: Animals in 'Mutiny' Fiction," *Journal of Victorian Culture* 17, no. 4 (2012): 480.
38. Hugh Ryan, "Why So Many Disney Villains Sound Gay," *Vice*, July 14, 2015, www.vice.com/en_ca/article/5g9e4d/the-number-of-gay-animated-villains-will-surprise-you-456. Noël Sturgeon has also argued that "the figure of the evil male homosexual often inhabits the ecovillains" of popular environmentally themed children's films, including Disney's *The Lion King*; Scar of that film is a clear descendent of Shere Khan. Sturgeon, *Environmentalism in Popular Culture: Gender, Race, Sexuality, and the Politics of the Natural* (Tucson: University of Arizona Press, 2009), 111.
39. Here, we can't help but recall that *other* flamboyantly queer tiger handler, Roy Horn of Siegfried and Roy, who died of COVID-19 a few weeks after the premiere of *Tiger King*, and who survived a gruesome tiger attack just like Joe Exotic's genderqueer employee Kelci "Saff" Saffery. A 2008 book about the pair, *The Secret Life of Siegfried and Roy: How the Tiger Kings Tamed Las Vegas*, by Jimmy Lavery et al., may have inspired the title of the program in question.
40. Stacy Gillis, "Sin and a Tiger Skin: The Stickiness of Elinor Glyn's *Three Weeks*," *Women: A Cultural Review* 29, no. 2 (2018): 218, 229.
41. Lindsay Albanese, "HOW TO WEAR ANIMAL PRINT (and look classy!)," YouTube, October 19, 2019, video, 6:48, https://youtu.be/c6M5sbWA4_Y; "How to Wear Animal Prints at Any Age," *Fabulous After 40*, n.d., www.fabulousafter40.com/how-to-wear-animal-prints-at-any-age/
42. "Visitor Demographics," *Association of Zoos and Aquariums*, n.d., www.aza.org/partnerships-visitor-demographics. The popularity of zoos sits in a mutually reinforcing relationship with television, with the zoo a common setting for wildlife programming from *Zoo Parade* onward. *The Secret Life of the Zoo* (2016–), for instance, filmed by Channel 4 in the UK's Chester Zoo and narrated successively by popular British actors Olivia Colman and Tamsin Grieg, has run for nine seasons.

43. Irus Braverman, *Zooland: The Institution of Captivity* (Stanford, CA: Stanford University Press, 2013), 158.
44. Ibid., 32.
45. Ibid., 43.
46. "Tigers," *U.S. Fish and Wildlife Service*, n.d., www.fws.gov/international/animals/tigers.html. Questions remain over the ethics and actual conservation value of zoos keeping animals in captivity, not least when zoos rarely contribute animals to reintroduction efforts and most reintroductions fail. See Mark R. Stanley Price and John E. Fa, "Reintroductions from Zoos: A Conservation Guiding Light or a Shooting Star?," in *Zoos in the 21st Century: Catalysts for Conservation?*, eds. Alexandra Zimmermann, Matthew Hatchwell, Leslie A. Dickie, and Chris West (Cambridge: Cambridge University Press, 2007), 166–7.
47. William G. Conway, "Buying Time for Wild animals with Zoos," *Zoo Biology* 30, no. 1 (2010).
48. On this rhetoric, and on other functions of time in the zoo, see Marianna Szczygielska, *Queer(ing) Naturecultures: The Study of Zoo Animals*, 2017, Central European University, Ph.D. dissertation, chapter 3, www.etd.ceu.edu/2017/szczygielska_marianna.pdf
49. In drawing attention to the relationship between time and the ethics of animal captivity, we draw on Dinesh Wadiwel, who has recently reframed the injustices of industrial animal agriculture in terms of the "working day" and curtailed life span of farmed animals. Wadiwel, "The Working Day: Animals, Capital and Surplus Time," in *Animal Labour: A New Frontier of Interspecies Justice?*, eds. Charlotte E. Blattner, Kendra Coulter, and Will Kymlicka (Oxford: Oxford University Press, 2020).
50. On the experience of time in prison, see Thomas Meisenhelder, "An Essay on Time and the Phenomenology of Imprisonment," *Deviant Behavior* 6, no. 1 (1985). On zoo and prison comparisons, see Braverman, *Zooland*, 86–9.
51. Nicole Seymour, *Strange Natures: Futurity, Empathy, and the Queer Ecological Imagination* (Urbana: University of Illinois Press, 2013), 7.
52. It is noteworthy in the context of the COVID-19 pandemic that heavy restrictions on direct animal contact in AZA-accredited zoos exist in part due to the risk of spreading zoonotic disease. On no contact, see Braverman, *Zooland*, 66, 147. On the dynamic of protection and violence in our orientation to the "cute," see Sianne Ngai, *Our Aesthetic Categories: Zany, Cute, Interesting* (Cambridge, MA: Harvard University Press, 2012), Chapter 1.
53. The AZA website records that "93% [of surveyed visitors] agree their family enjoys seeing animals up close at zoos and aquariums" and "94% feel that zoos and aquariums teach children about how people can protect animals and the habitats they depend on." "Visitor Demographics."
54. Bonnie Hallman and S. Mary P. Benbow, "Family Leisure, Family Photography and Zoos: Exploring the Emotional Geographies of Families," *Social & Cultural Geography* 8, no. 6 (2007): 871.
55. Elizabeth Freeman, *Time Binds: Queer Temporalities, Queer Histories* (Durham and London: Duke University Press, 2010), XXII.
56. Harlan Weaver, "Pit Bull Promises: Inhuman Intimacies and Queer Kinships in an Animal Shelter," *GLQ* 21, nos. 2–3 (2015): 352, 343.
57. Gay animals have recently become a popular zoo and documentary novelty, particularly gay penguins. The draw of these animals is largely based on their participation in a homonormative narrative of pair bonding and

reproduction. See, for instance, Liam Stack, "Gay Penguins, and Their Hope for a Baby, Have Enchanted Berlin," *New York Times*, August 14, 2019, www.nytimes.com/2019/08/14/world/europe/male-penguins-adoption-egg-berlin-zoo.html. Alternately, as Cynthia Chris points out, gay animal behavior is often portrayed in wildlife documentaries as evidence of sexual immaturity. Chris, *Watching Wildlife* (Minneapolis, MN: University of Minnesota Press, 2006), 125.

58. Ibid., 124.
59. See Nicole Seymour, *Bad Environmentalism: Irony and Irreverence in the Ecological Age* (Minneapolis, MN: University of Minnesota Press, 2018), Chapter 2.
60. Barbara Crowther, "Viewing What Comes Naturally: A Feminist Approach to Television Natural History," *Women's Studies International Forum* 20, no. 2 (1997): 295.
61. Amy Watson, "Netflix Subscriptions in the U.S. 2020, by Generation," *Statistica*, May 28, 2020, www.statista.com/statistics/720723/netflix-members-usa-by-age-group/
62. Hannah Yelin, "Tiger King Is Popular Because We Love to Laugh at 'White Trash' – Here's Why That's Dangerous," *The Independent*, April 8, 2020, www.independent.co.uk/voices/tiger-king-netflix-joe-exotic-carole-baskin-eugenics-zoo-a9454491.html
63. Susan Murray, "'I Think We Need a New Name for It': The Meeting of Documentary and Reality TV," in *Reality TV: Remaking Television Culture*, eds. Susan Murray and Laurie Ouellette (New York: New York University Press, 2004), 65–81.
64. Ibid., 41.
65. Tom Skinner, "'Tiger King' Co-Creator Says Racism from Joe Exotic Was Cut from Documentary," *NME*, April 7, 2020, www.nme.com/news/tv/tiger-king-joe-exotic-racism-cut-from-show-2642740
66. Michelle Alexander, *The New Jim Crow: Mass Incarceration in the Age of Colorblindness* (New York: The New Press, 2010), 18.
67. This pattern of thought, as Zakiyyah Iman Jackson notes, is not restricted to far-right ideology but built into the structures of European humanism. Jackson, *Becoming Human: Matter and Meaning in an Anti-Black World* (New York: New York University Press, 2020), 4. A number of recent works in Black Studies have taken on the fraught relationship between Black and animal activist movements and the troubling analogues between Black and animal experience frequently made in the context of animal advocacy, including Jackson's *Becoming Human*, Joshua Bennett, *Being Property Once Myself: Blackness and the End of Man* (Cambridge, MA: Belknap Press, 2020), and Bénédicte Boisseron, *Afro-Dog: Blackness and the Animal Question* (New York: Columbia University Press, 2018). For an overview of the core debates, see Ibid., Chapter 1.
68. Kristy Puchko, "Trixie Mattel and Katya Review 'Tiger King'," *Pajiba*, July 1, 2020, www.pajiba.com/tv_reviews/drag-queens-trixie-mattel-and-katya-review-tiger-king.php
69. Libby Torres, "Everything We Know About the Competing 'Tiger King' Adaptations, Which Reportedly Star Nicolas Cage and Kate McKinnon," *Insider*, May 5, 2020, www.insider.com/tiger-king-remake-adaptations-nicolas-cage-kate-mckinnon-2020-5

70. Eric Todisco, "Tiger King Fans Flock to Joe Exotic's Zoo for Its Reopening After Coronavirus Shutdown," *People*, May 6, 2020, https://people.com/pets/tiger-king-fans-crowd-joe-exotic-zoo-reopening-coronavirus/; Miranda Bryant, "Tiger King Zoo Closes Suddenly After License Suspended," *The Guardian*, August 19, 2020, www.theguardian.com/media/2020/aug/19/oklahoma-zoo-tiger-king-closes-suddenly-after-license-suspended

71. Harvey Hawkins (@harvhawkscomedy), "Can't Believe It's Nearly Lockdown Again Already: Swear It Gets Earlier and Earlier Every Year: I Walked Past a House Earlier and He Was Already," *Twitter*, September 11, 2020, https://twitter.com/harvhawkscomedy/status/1304483781160701952?lang=en-gb

2 Netflix's docuseries style

Generic chaos and affect in *Tiger King*

Jorie Lagerwey and Taylor Nygaard

A *Variety* headline from December 2019 reported that "Netflix Released More Originals in 2019 Than the Entire [U.S.] TV Industry did in 2005."[1] *The Verge* was even more direct six months later with its headline, "Netflix is Straight Up Flexing at This Point."[2] It can be hard to determine exactly how much of the streaming platform's enormous productivity is in its documentary division, but it is fair to say it outpaces its competitors.[3] Sudeep Sharma suggests that documentaries are "a core pillar of its [Netflix's] service, both as a way to highlight its connection to quality cinema and to distinguish its catalog from more mundane forms of television programming."[4] While its documentary feature productions like *American Factory* and *My Octopus Teacher* may win Oscars (Best Documentary Feature in 2020 and 2021, respectively) and by extension prestige for the brand, Netflix's docuseries also generate remarkable buzz and viewing numbers.[5] Boosted by pandemic lockdowns that sent record numbers of people to streaming platforms to pass the time,[6] *Tiger King: Murder, Mayhem and Madness* (Netflix 2020) had 34 million viewers worldwide in its first ten days[7] and 64 million in its first month.[8] A 2020 year-end press release from the streamer celebrated its original nonfiction content:

> We escaped the shutdown through the reality of other people's lives: We spent twice as much time watching documentaries and reality TV this year than last year. Our top docuseries were *Tiger King* and *Killer Inside: The Mind of Aaron Hernandez* and our most successful documentary features were *American Murder: The Family Next Door* and *The Social Dilemma*. On the reality TV side, *Floor is Lava, Love is Blind* and *Too Hot To Handle* were our most popular releases of the year.[9]

The variety of these nonfiction hits reflects the supposed media personalization of Netflix's brand – there's nonfiction content for everyone. But, despite the seeming variety, there's a certain consistency across Netflix docuseries

DOI: 10.4324/9781003157205-3

that emerges from the demands that its branding, extensive output, and production schedules place on producers. This chapter uses *Tiger King* as a case study to examine Netflix's house style for docuseries: a style that relies on what we call "generic chaos," with closer ties to reality television than feature documentary production practices, and a resultant emphasis on affective characterization and viewer reactions over intellectual engagement or investigation. Partially a product of Netflix's commercial mandate, this house style results in a tendency for Netflix's docuseries in general, and *Tiger King* in particular, to other its main characters by framing them in an affective mode that forecloses the empathy promised by documentary's frequent positioning as edifying or socially and politically engaged.

At its root, genre is an organizing principle; it is a way to categorize texts in any medium. It may be used by the entertainment industry for marketing, branding, or audience targeting; by creators to structure their ideas into saleable commodities; by audiences to choose what to watch; or by critics and scholars to understand the cultural and ideological functions of genres that are popular in a given historical moment. Because genres involve patterns of narrative, characterization, and visual and aural iconography, their repetition can be comforting, or at least predictable. Lauren Berlant has written about viewers' emotional relation to familiar genres, arguing that "Genres provide an affective expectation of the experience of watching something unfold, whether that thing is in life or in art."[10] In other words, viewers become so accustomed to generic patterns that when art or even real life does not conform to those expected patterns, they may be bitterly disappointed and experience the affect she calls "cruel optimism." While cruel optimism is not the specific affect we see operating in *Tiger King* or in Netflix's docuseries productions more broadly, the important point is that expectations about genres have consequences far beyond the text, in viewers' lived experience and affective responses. As Jason Mittell argues, television genres are cultural (rather than merely textual) categories encompassing "industry, audience, and cultural practices as well."[11] We make these points not only to illustrate the importance of genre study but also to help recognize the significance, far beyond textual analysis, of altering, hybridizing, or experimenting with genre. As we lay out the features of generic chaos below, it will become clear that affect – of both characterization or representation and targeted viewer reactions – is central to Netflix's house style. And because of Netflix's massive output of documentaries, the company has an outsized impact on the development, visibility, and understanding of the genre in the early 21st century.

Tiger King is marketed as an "American true crime documentary series."[12] True crime has surged in popularity, especially in serialized formats, since the hit podcast *Serial*'s first season in 2014. Tanya Horeck details the proliferation and popularity of serialized true crime since the podcast's debut, suggesting that since *Serial*'s buzzy viral hit status, there's been an increasing number of blockbuster true crime serials including *The Jinx* (HBO 2015), Netflix's own *Making a Murderer* (Netflix 2015–18), and now *Tiger King*. Horeck also observes that the docuseries (as opposed to the documentary feature) borrows the structure of seriality from reality television soap operas (sometimes called docusoaps).[13] Although reality television is a malleable, fluid concept, it is often characterized by "hybrid genres that were previously discrete, blurring the lines between [for example] documentary journalism and glitzy entertainment."[14] Describing some of the most popular reality television programming in the early 2000s, Ron Simon argues that one of the defining features of reality television docusoaps – especially in comparison to the verité documentaries that had aired on television prior – was their "immediacy, a seemingly present-tense quality to the narrative . . . the pleasure based on the unpredictability of the outcome."[15] With *Tiger King*, like a lot of popular true crime serials, the immediacy and collective viewing or listening experience generated by a viral smash hit pairs well with soapy seriality to emphasize affective audience reactions over documentary's more traditional "sober discourse."[16] *Serial*'s first season, which reinvestigated the 1999 murder case against then-teenaged Adnan Syed, is a good example. The story unfolded over 12 episodes released weekly, unveiling analysis of evidence and new interviews week by week, complete with teasers and cliffhangers at the end of each episode. The serial strategy, emphasized by the title, was extremely effective in creating a "must-listen" pop culture phenomenon. Furthermore, the primary journalist and host, Sarah Koenig, and her podcast producers inserted themselves in the story, frequently discussing their feelings about the case and their very personalized emotional reactions, especially to the imprisoned Syed who just seemed too nice to have murdered anyone. As Horeck notes, *Serial* was the first true crime serial blockbuster, and the melodramatic tools it used to create suspense and emotional engagement became a template for the contemporary genre. Netflix learned from *Serial* and others that an affective reaction triggers the binge reflex that Netflix and its fellow streamers require to keep viewers subscribed. As Mareike Jenner argues, these strategies are an explicit component of Netflix's original programming development process.[17]

Lisa Nishimura, vice president of independent film and documentary features at Netflix, has been in charge of greenlighting documentaries for the streamer for over a decade and was ultimately responsible for Netflix's development of *Tiger King*.[18] On hearing the initial pitch, she was immediately interested in *Tiger King* because of its parallels with *Making a Murderer*, another Netflix surprise hit she had been responsible for greenlighting. Both nonfiction series had a basis in the popular true crime genre, and their focus on rural American Whiteness provided a spectacle of otherness for Netflix-viewing demographics.[19] Nishimura championed both series to go on longer than many critics and audiences deemed necessary, with *Making*'s contrived second season featuring a highly telegenic new lawyer, and *Tiger King*'s rushed, added-on eighth episode filmed after the series' outsized success.[20] Drawing out a profitable series is a common business practice in a relatively conservative TV industry that favors repetition over experimentation. Spin-off series, new shows based on a popular secondary character of an existing successful show, are a tried-and-true example of the industry's preference for keeping existing audiences with more of the same rather than taking the larger financial risk of greenlighting an entirely new creative project with as yet unproven audience appeal. Genre itself is another such risk-averse business practice. True crime is one contemporary iteration of a genre that, given one or two hit instantiations, has suddenly flourished and proliferated. Earlier examples of this pattern include Westerns in 1960s and 1970s US television schedules and docusoaps in the wake of the 2007 Writers Guild of America strike and the resultant boom in so-called unscripted reality television.[21] In addition to genre and subject matter, Netflix has determined that cultivating affective characterizations and serial narrative structures within true crime will produce a bingeable and therefore bankable product.

Many years before *Tiger King* was purchased by Netflix, it was loosely conceived of as an exploratory episodic docuseries for CNN about exotic animal owners. The project morphed over time: from a "big cat" film to a three-episode series to the eventual seven-episode serial it became at Netflix.[22] Netflix's quantitative imperative – that is, its need for a constant stream of newness to maintain subscriber interest and avoid subscription churn – forced the already long-running production away from a cohesive, concise documentary and toward reality television's generic hybridity, affective immediacy, and production practices. At least in part because of that quantitative imperative, Netflix docuseries favor reality TV production practices and reality soaps' affective payoffs over true crime's slower, more carefully constructed investigatory mode or more traditional documentary's pro-social sober discourses.[23] Exemplifying this focus on affect, Episode 5 of *Tiger King* features the tragic, apparently accidental, suicide of protagonist Joe Exotic's husband, Travis Maldonado. The death itself is captured via security camera footage not of Travis, who is standing out of frame directly under the wall-mounted camera, but of Joshua Dial, Joe's gubernatorial campaign manager. Josh is seated in an office chair in a cluttered warehouse, facing an offscreen Travis, and he is narrating the events through a combination of intercut interview footage (shot inexplicably, and with alienating effect, outdoors in front of a chicken coop) and voice over the surveillance video. The surveillance footage itself is silent, so we cannot see or hear the gunshot. But, the graininess and angle of this footage pretend at a passive observational mode and offer verité authenticity to Josh's, and by extension the viewer's, reactions to Travis' death. Rather than the gunshot, we see Josh's mouth go wide in a sudden gasp as he clasps his hands to the sides of his face and remains frozen in that posture for approximately 25 seconds. The timecode on the surveillance camera does the work of offering authenticity and immediacy to the event while also capturing the witness's stunned shock and delayed movement. In interview footage recalling the event and its aftermath, Josh reveals "I felt like I was attached to Joe by pain. Like we had a bond of pain" over Travis's death. The local news footage of Joe sobbing, hands covering his face, while an unidentified man offers comfort, alongside supporting interviews from zoo staff, bolsters the narrative of authenticity surrounding Joe's grief. Respect for Joe's loss is further reflected in the framing, which is more distant, and the performances, which are much quieter and appear private rather than staged for a presumed viewing audience. Similarly, a subsequent scene in which Joe provides Thanksgiving dinner for the whole community is filmed from a distance, in a more observational visual language than the rest of the series. This particular scene illustrates the rationale behind Nishimura's decision to buy *Tiger King*: "When I took the original meeting with the filmmakers and we started talking about the subjects and the materials they had, it struck me that they had an enormous amount of access and that a lot of it was verité. So, it's not meant to be someone telling you how to feel."[24] Nishimura here invokes the strong observational tradition of verité documentary and the idea of a neutral observer filmmaker giving the audience interpretive agency. Nishimura's framing attempts to position *Tiger King* in a highbrow tradition of sober documentary and intellectually engaged viewing. However, the series' heavy reliance on found footage intentionally shot for a never-realized reality TV show, and participant interviews in environments precisely stage-managed to frame their subjects as eccentric or bizarre, contradict that view and illustrate the amalgam of true crime and reality television that the series is.

That mix creates the extreme generic hybridization we call generic chaos. In contrast to the relatively consistent verité style of the scenes just described, the first 60 seconds of *Tiger King* offers a better example of the series' style as it mashes up elements of true crime, soap opera, local news, and even the Hollywood Western. The opening sequence begins with an interview with jaded reality TV producer Rick Kirkham, decked out in a wide brim hat and chain-smoking cigarettes like a cross between Humphrey Bogart and Crocodile Dundee. So the opening shots alone reference genres and modes ranging from reality TV and noir to nostalgic 1980s camp. Next, a series of archival clips (a traditional documentary technique) shows big cats as owner's pets, including a full-grown lion riding in the passenger seat of a convertible. An interview with zookeeper John Reinke is next up, and the ideologically laden mise-en-scène, featuring a tiger skin on the wall and a holstered gun on the sofa beside him, belies any documentary objectivity in favor of reality TV style sensationalism. Next, a series of decades-old still photos of characters who will appear in subsequent episodes is followed by local news narration that serves as voiceover to a crane shot of Joe Exotic (who has not yet been introduced) walking along a dirt road between metal enclosures at his zoo. Several shots show tigers pacing within those enclosures before we see a close-up of Joe Exotic's mid-section, featuring glitter-encrusted handcuffs, a low-slung Wild West style hip holster, and Joe's hands spinning the cylinder of his pistol before slotting it home. In this first minute alone, the series mixes sensationalist staging and set design with tropes and conventions of a chaotic mix of genres. Throughout the remaining seven episodes of the series, the list of generic referents, practices, and qualities only grows, producing a messy generic recombination that evokes docusoap melodrama, true crime investigation, verité emotional authenticity, tabloid TV spectacle, and anthropological voyeurism, among others. This recombinant style has the adeptness to say many things to many audiences, contributing to its mass appeal despite increasing audience fragmentation and nichification of audiences' viewing habits. The generic chaos also cultivates a targeted reaction from the audience that privileges affective reactions over intellectual engagement or investigation.

Tiger King's extreme generic hybridity needs to be understood in the broad cultural context of what Lynne Joyrich calls the "reality televisualization" of politics and public life. Reality televisualization "is a kind of televisual epistemology and a televisual affect intertwined, a meshing of modes of thinking and modes of feeling, which has become the 'medium' in which our politics now exist."[25] Her theory helps elucidate how citizens have started to see, understand, and react to political discourse primarily in affective terms.[26] This broader cultural shift away from reasoned assessments of shared facts toward individualized emotional responses to current events is mirrored in generic transformations. Perhaps surprisingly, documentary, and specifically true crime documentary – a genre allegedly about investigation and fact finding rather than individual opinion or emotional intensity – has spiked in popularity and sheer quantity of productions in this environment of streaming and personalized viewing schedules that parallels the individuality of political discourse. Horeck argues that it is the specific technological affordances of digital streaming platforms and their participatory social media accompaniments that make affective responses to true crime primary. She writes that "there is a continual interpellation of the viewer into sensational 'money shot' displays of affective response and reaction."[27] Despite the reference to pornography, this move toward the sensational is more in line with reality TV than true crime or other documentary subgenres. Shocking moments happen in nearly every episode of *Tiger King*. In Episode 2, for example, zookeeper Saff is attacked by a tiger and subsequently rushed to the hospital where his arm is amputated. In Episode 3, the show suddenly suggests Carole Baskin murdered her first husband and fed him to her tigers, an unsubstantiated claim that disappears again after this episode. Most shocking and horrific of all, as mentioned previously, in Episode 5, Joe's husband Travis Maldonado accidentally takes his own life by shooting himself with a gun he thought was disabled. Each of these moments evokes emotional or even physical (exclaiming, laughing, crying) responses from viewers in the manner of what Linda Williams describes as "body genres" like melodrama, horror, and pornography, which elicit similar physical bodily reactions from viewers.[28] The unrelenting pace of those moments and the reactions they elicit are a result of Netflix's reality televisualization of the true crime docuseries – a process that begins behind the scenes long before audiences consume and react to the images.

Tiger King's shooting and editing process, described by series editor Doug Abel, paints a picture much more akin to reality TV production practices than feature production and thus helps explain its generic transformation and resultant solicitation of affect. Feature documentary productions typically work from a detailed script or plan (albeit a flexible one to allow for potential revelations from interviewees or the process of investigation during filming), have the unifying vision of a single director or directorial team, and generally (especially in the investigatory or true crime modes) have a clear narrative arc and argument. In contrast, reality TV production is designed for speed and volume. Story lines may be suggested, and scenes even staged by producers on set, but ultimately editors create story from vast hours of footage that is submitted as it is taken during what could be months of filming. Editors then are responsible for sifting through all the video and cobbling together conflicts and resolutions for weekly episodes. Because this unscripted footage rarely conforms to television's favorite narrative pattern of situation/disruption or conflict/resolution, reality soaps borrow instead from scripted soaps' emphasis on emotional drama, details of mundane life, and changes in characters' relationships over time. Furthermore, as with most television production, reality TV shows are rarely the product of a single director, but rather a stable of directors working from production guidelines; footage is sometimes further collected by automated, constantly running cameras, monitoring participants in specific spaces.

Abel describes shaping Joe Exotic's story on the fly, as footage arrived and without a script, inventing or discovering story lines based on available footage in much the same way a reality TV show would. A large team of editors (again more akin to reality television than feature practices) worked on particular episodes individually. But at the same time, they were all cutting new footage as it arrived and new information came in. Often, multiple editors would take a pass at each episode, Abel said, each bringing their unique perspectives to the footage and potentially altering the focus or vision of the previous editor. Further complicating the editorial disorganization, Netflix gave the production a hard deadline of November 2019, despite the fact that "lots of material was slowly leaking in from different drives and sources" throughout the editing process. Because of this hard deadline, "they weren't able to bring a lot of stories to a full conclusion. . . . [We] had a hard deadline and reverse engineered it from there." Abel describes the last few months of editing as a "mad scramble," with the resulting story like a "Russian doll," with every story line opening up to reveal another and yet another nested inside but lacking the time to follow any one of them through. This report suggests that the generic chaos seen onscreen was not a conscious choice but a result of cultural, industrial, and ultimately pragmatic factors.

The lack of planning and writing is explicit in onscreen conversations between directors Rebecca Chaiklin and Eric Goode, reflecting their own affective response as well. Chaiklin says, in reference to a federal investigation into Joe's murder-for-hire plot, "Oh my god. I can't believe. . . . I mean it was sort of funny when they started, but it's gotten really dark" (Episode 5). In an interview with *The Washington Post*, Chaiklin notes,

> We wanted to tell the story of what was happening behind the curtain in these roadside zoos. And it became very evident pretty quickly that it was much more captivating and would reach a wider audience to tell it from the people who were involved with it as opposed to the activists, the sanctuary people, who would go on a diatribe about the horrors of it, which was actually quite uninteresting and really not very good on screen.[29]

Chaiklin is explicit about the choice to emphasize emotional investment in character over narrative structure or social problem documentary argumentation. Chaiklin's description of *Tiger King* as ambiguously "funny" is also significant to our understanding of the effects of generic chaos. Genres that are obviously comedic like sitcoms play with identification by pointing a viewer's laughter either *at* or *with* unlikeable characters.[30] Tanya Horeck extends that idea to true crime, arguing that *The Jinx* establishes " 'a comic modality,' which, as Geoff King suggests, 'permit(s) the viewer to remain detached, to enjoy the spectacle of violent antics without any feeling of implication, of having to 'care' very much about the consequences."[31] The comic modality in *Tiger King* is created in part by the otherworldly spectacle of the tigers and other exotic animals that roam the background of the series both narratively and visually. It is heightened by Joe Exotic's outsized performance and narcissistic drive for visibility, as evidenced by his homemade reality show, his self-produced music videos, his mullet hairstyle, and the fact that he slings his pistol like an outlaw in a Western rather than a 21st-century zookeeper. In other words, even his choice of gun is performative and seems tinged with kitsch, not entirely unlike the line of self-designed underwear sold in the zoo's gift shop.

We've argued elsewhere that *Tiger King*'s paratexts – like its promotional material, user-generated memes, and other social media discourses, as well as the extra interview episode of the series hosted by satiric talk show host Joel McHale – encourage a glib, gawking viewing position for the docuseries.[32] Countless reviews introduced the series with a similarly gawping tone: "Like a car accident on a freeway, *Tiger King* is a mess that you can't look away from."[33] As *The Atlantic*'s Sophie Gilbert writes,

> There are no heroes in *Tiger King*. Not Joseph "Joe Exotic" Maldonado-Passage, whose stripy mullet you've surely seen on social media, accompanied by a teal sequined jacket so ostentatious that the adult tiger he's posing with looks like an afterthought. Not Bhagavan "Doc" Antle, who, one former employee alleges, coerces teenage girls working 100-hour weeks at his ranch to reach "his level of enlightenment" by sleeping with him. . . . And definitely not Eric Goode, the New York hotelier and animal-rights activist who co-directed the series, whose elevator pitch for it seems to have been "What if Christopher Guest, but real?" and whose disdain for the dentally challenged and leopard-print-festooned characters he captures is *Tiger King*'s most discernible emotion.[34]

The popularity of *Tiger King* in a high-stakes election year after "anger and laughter provide[d] progressives with different opportunities to weather, make fun of, and combat the ascendancy of right-wing populism," defines the affective complexity of the cultural moment.[35]

Furthermore, throughout 2020, when viewers were watching *Tiger King* in droves, both the COVID-19 pandemic and the increased visibility and support for the Black Lives Matter movement after the murder of George Floyd by police sparked new conversations about empathy. From popular press accounts to memes and YouTube videos to academic articles and memoirs, cries for renewed or reconceptualized understandings of empathy circulated broadly, suggesting that "America is a country in deep pain."[36] In an era when these crises are compounding the economic insecurity, political polarization, misinformation, and general daily uncertainty dominating Americans' lives, many activists urged increased compassion for each other. Reflecting on the parallel public health crises of the pandemic and anti-Black racism, political scientist Terri E. Givens used her personal experience and expertise in higher education to advocate for "radical empathy."[37] She argues that this form of anti-racist activism requires moving beyond an understanding of others' lives to understand the origins of our biases. It requires not only adopting the perspective of others but also taking action to combat injustice. Her understanding of empathy parallels Brené Brown's. A scholar of emotions and popular author (and star of a Netflix special, *Brené Brown: The Call to Courage*, 2019) she breaks down an important distinction between empathy (feeling with) and sympathy (feeling for): "Empathy fuels connection, sympathy drives disconnection,"[38] she says. Empathy is about "perspective taking" and "staying out of judgement," about recognizing and communicating back to someone their feelings. For Brown and many others who have mobilized empathy for social justice politics, empathy is a practice of "feeling with people," which requires vulnerability, "getting down into someone's pain or experience," alongside them, and which rejects the distance conjured by sympathy. At its best, documentary's realism has the potential to cultivate empathy from viewers with its subjects, occasionally even leading to real-world actions or activism from viewers. Discussing narrative empathy in the film *Tongues Untied* (1989), for example, Leah Anderst traces how intense identification with characters is thought to produce in viewers a greater understanding of another's perspective or positive changes in their own thinking.[39] Tanya Horeck further suggests that crime documentaries specifically "often circulate in the public sphere as objects of emotion – whipping up social outrage by campaigning against wrongful criminal convictions, or exposing gross injustices (for example, *The Thin Blue Line* [Morris, US, 1988] and the *Paradise Lost* trilogy [Berlinger and Sinofsky, US, 1996, 2000 and 2012])."[40] This exhortation to empathy, however, and the potential for documentary to mobilize that potentially prosocial affect exist simultaneously in our current moment within Joyrich's reality televisualization of culture. The "meshing of modes of thinking and feeling" alongside reality TV's emphasis on shock and the eliciting of immediate intense viewer reaction reflected in *Tiger King*'s production practices means that evoking empathy is far from straightforward.

While Givens argues for the urgent necessity of radical empathy to achieve social justice and Horeck illustrates that true crime in particular is a subgenre of affect, Anderst notes a crucial caveat:

Experiencing empathy, a viewer can impose her ideas or reactions onto the experiences or emotions of another in the belief that what she experiences is what they experienced. It is for this reason that Sara Ahmed calls empathy, especially empathy for another's pain, a "wish feeling," a phenomenon "in which subjects 'feel' something other than what another feels in the very moment of imagining they could feel what another feels."[41]

Extending this possible disconnect between viewer and subject "feelings," Lisa Nakamura says that documentaries can produce a "a spurious or 'toxic empathy' that enables White viewers to feel that they have experienced authentic empathy for these others."[42] In other words, it allows viewers to "feel good about feeling bad" without inspiring the vulnerable, radical, perspective taking empathy advocated by Brown and Givens.[43] While *Tiger King* traverses politically charged subject matter like rural poverty, queerness, addiction, disability, sexual exploitation, and animal rights while featuring a cast of potentially empathetic characters, its aesthetic structure – its generic chaos – dominates and dilutes any potential for radical empathy and works instead in the "comic modality" Horeck posited for *The Jinx*.

Episode 2 of *Tiger King* provides a template for how the series takes high-stakes affective events and, by stringing them together at a rapid-fire pace that denies the viewer time to process or the narrative time to investigate, focuses on shock and reactivity instead of allowing the viewer to experience "radical empathy." Like the opening 60 seconds of the series described previously, Episode 2 contains at least three themes or story lines that are never followed through to a conclusion. The episode opens in the language of tabloid style reality TV with a recorded 911 call reporting a tiger attack on zookeeper Saff, whose arm has been bitten nearly off; it is later amputated in the hospital. Saff, who is transgender and continuously misgendered by Joe as well as the film (an error, or a possible cruelty made explicit by the 911 caller correctly gendering him), represents one instance of the potential for radical empathy. A personable, non-White trans man who experienced violent trauma leading to permanent disability is a naturally sympathetic character. This event, like many others in the series, operates within what Laura Grindstaff and Susan Murray call "the 'emotional economy' of contemporary reality television." They argue that "Reality television derives its claim to the real by spotlighting the emotional expressiveness of ordinary people and branding this expressiveness as a signifier of both individuals and the genre as a whole."[44] As a hybrid of reality television and true crime, the series opens further potential for a more complex representation of living confidently and comfortably with disability – a representation that might cultivate radical empathy – when it cuts from Saff's story to John Reinke's. A double amputee whose prosthetic legs are painted with scary clown faces in which he clearly delights, Reinke briefly tells his story. But rather than developing this theme, Reinke's story is included essentially only to clarify that he was not the victim of a tiger attack. Disability is never mentioned again.

The same episode then cuts from this story line (further sensationalized with clips from contemporary news coverage like CNN's "Tiger Mauls Zoo Keeper" interview with Joe) to Doc Antle, the owner of another exotic animal zoo, riding into frame for the first time astride an elephant strolling down a Myrtle Beach, South Carolina street. The "comic modality" here is created by the bizarre clash between elephant and quiet American neighborhood. The character introduction is designed to startle viewers with its out-of-place elephant, situating yet another character as an eccentric to goggle and possibly laugh at. The off-balance sensation cultivated by elephant-in-suburbia is heightened by the sequence that follows, featuring Carole Baskin, John Finlay, and Mario Tabruae. Baskin's breathy voice and penchant for animal print clothing and flowers in her hair open her to sartorial ridicule regardless of what she's saying, and Joe's constant aggressive name-calling, derisive imitation, and elaborately planned threats to murder her, continuously undermine empathy for her. Finlay is sympathetic, but always filmed shirtless, making the viewer wonder why convention has been broken in this way rather than focusing on his words. (In the final Q&A episode, he explains he was simply proud of his tattoos and wanted to show them off.) Tabruae is another potentially humanized exotic animal zoo owner, but he is introduced as an ex-drug lord famous for being the alleged source material for the main character in Brian DePalma's hyper-violent 1983 gangster film *Scarface*. This criminal past is irrelevant to any action in *Tiger King* but offers yet another shock payoff in the "emotional economy" of the series.

This episode also introduces us to Barbara Fisher, a former "apprentice" to Doc Antle. While she says she will always love him, her interview paints a picture of Antle as a controlling, manipulative sexual predator. Significantly, the score throughout this sequence is bouncy and bright instead of somber and threatening, pushing the viewer toward interpreting this as side-show fun rather than scandal. The repetition of photographs of heavily made-up, skinny, sexily outfitted young women workers at Antle's zoo, the fact that as many as nine teenagers who arrived to work as extremely low-paid "apprentices" "stayed on," in Antle's words, to become his wives is again played to provoke bemused astonishment rather than to investigate criminal sexual coercion. This opens another potential theme in this episode of the appalling labor conditions at all these exotic animal zoos. Again, rather than allowing that theme to develop, it degenerates into a voyeuristic spectacle of poverty porn – the relishing in visually excessive displays of poverty – when Joe's employees discuss eating from the "meat truck." Expired and other meat products not suitable for sale at Walmart are delivered to the zoo to feed the animals, but the staff, paid so little they often cannot afford food, take the best or least out-of-date meat for themselves first. The visual excess comes from zoo employees dumping enormous trash cans of processed meat products from the back of a truck and from images of mounds of raw meat piled in a dumpster. In the midst of the spectacle, Eric Cowie, cigarette dangling from his mouth, exclaims that a package of something he's found is still frozen and that he'll "take that home." In the same scene, an unnamed zoo employee goofs around in the meat truck with a long string of something like beef jerky dangling from his mouth as he chews. This silly moment ends the scene, again emphasizing humor at the individual performance rather than empathy with or even outrage over the poverty and exploitation all these workers face.

This emphasis on humor over empathy is particularly problematic because the cast contains an array of marginalized characters. Some are rural and poor (everyone affiliated with Joe's zoo while it is under his control); experiencing or recovering from addiction (John Finlay, Eric Cowie); disabled (Saff and John Reinke); expressing queer sexualities (Joe, his husbands Travis Maldonado and John Finlay, Joshua Dial); or nonbinary gender (Saff). But, the show's chaotic structure, lack of coherent narrative, and insistence on continual emotional, "money shots" cultivate laughter *at* rather than empathy *with* these people. The combination of marketing *Tiger King* as a documentary series and the resultant invocations of truth claims, cultural value, and seriousness with the practices of a very different genre that values melodrama and spectacle above all troubles the cultural position of the program. The result is the potential for the affective reactions to otherness being read, via documentary, as factual rather than spectacular and othering. Furthermore, because bingeing requires affective investment, generic chaos is a house style Netflix consciously cultivates in order to integrate binge-watching into its brand identity.

One of the other most popular docuseries of 2020, *Killer Inside: The Mind of Aaron Hernandez*, is a further example of Netflix's documentary production practices and generic chaos. With similar positioning as true crime, *Killer Inside* presents itself as an examination of the life and murder trial of former NFL player Aaron Hernandez, as well as an indictment of chronic traumatic encephalopathy (CTE), a degenerative neurological condition attributed to multiple concussions. However, three hour-long episodes form a nonlinear jumble of accusations and insinuations about Hernandez's life, career, and crime. Like *Tiger King*, story lines are raised and dropped; assumptions are presented, but promised evidence never appears.

Most egregiously, Hernandez's sexuality is questioned via hearsay that suggests that Hernandez's possible homosexuality could be the reason he murdered his friend. To be clear, it is not presented as a motive for murder. Rather, it is presented as though homosexuality is a pathology on par with CTE and a potential trigger for unexplained murder. The generic confusion, muddled storytelling, and spectacularization of otherness in service of salacious escapism are the hallmarks of Netflix-produced docuseries, which we see in *Tiger King* as well.

Netflix's house style must be interrogated because of its massive production output, audience reach, and resultant influence on genre. Its overemphasis on affective reactions from viewers is particularly troubling in a time of media fragmentation, heightened individualism, and extreme political division. Social justice activists like Givens and Brown encourage radical empathy as one path to reconciliation in this time of compounding crises. In that context, the very large number of 64 million worldwide viewers recalls the mass viewing conditions and conciliatory potential of television as a "cultural forum."[45] In the same vein, documentary's sober discourse carries prestige, and its reputation for edification holds promise to inspire social justice activism. However, generic chaos and the comic modality of Netflix's docuseries house style disrupt that promise.

Furthermore, it is important to note that while Netflix's content is theoretically designed for diverse, heterogenous global audiences, the way its docuseries others characters who display difference, as we see in *Tiger King*, rather than cultivating empathy with them, suggests that its target audience is actually an elite audience with a shared class-based taste culture.[46] Discussing different modes of TV viewing during COVID-19 lockdowns in spring and summer 2020, television scholars Lynne Joyrich, Laurie Ouellette, and Herman Gray assert that the imagined community[47] of pandemic television viewers who were watching more streaming television programming than ever before remains intensely exclusionary; it presumes access to Whiteness, patriarchy, middle-classness, and heteronormativity. In particular, they argue that pandemic hits like *Tiger King, Killer Inside*, HBO's *The Vow*, and ESPN's *The Last Dance* spoke to audiences that excluded many essential workers who were forced to continue working through dangerous contagion. These essential workers, often pictured as doctors and nurses, also included postal workers and delivery people, grocery store clerks, and waste disposal workers: those working-class laborers who were earning far less than the white-collar workers who were able to transition to working from home. Ultimately, this simply highlights the TV industry's long-held definition of and focus on so-called "quality" audiences: the White, urban, and affluent – a demographic that Netflix openly courts.[48] And, while the centering of these elite audiences and content is not necessarily new, given the prominence and popularity of certain pandemic television hits, Gray asks an important related question: "Who in this [pandemic] moment do we [television audiences] get to care for?" Who are the subjects at the center of our stories; how are their stories framed, and for whom are those stories told? Reality televisualization and generic chaos in Netflix's docuseries lead to a detachment from characters by cultivating looking (and sometimes gawking) *at* rather than feeling *with*. As a product of its commercial mandate, branding, and production practices, Netflix's docuseries house style positions its characters as bizarre and invites spectators to ridicule them or dismiss them as mere spectacles. In doing so, it precludes empathetic identification – especially via the storytelling pattern that raises and then dismisses so many potentially radically empathetic issues around poverty, queerness, disability, sexual exploitation, and more. In Netflix docuseries like *Tiger King*, there is a lack of sustained intellectual engagement or investigation because of their reliance on reality television tropes and disorganized production. The result is a generic chaos that promotes affective characterization but not empathy at a time when mass television audiences might need it the most.

Notes

1. Gavin Bridge, "Netflix Released More Originals in 2019 Than the Entire TV Industry did in 2005," *Variety*, December 17, 2019, https://variety.com/2019/tv/news/netflix-more-2019-originals-than-entire-tv-industry-in-2005–1203441709/
2. Julia Alexander, "Netflix Is Straight Up Flexing at This Point," *The Verge*, June 24, 2020, www.theverge.com/2020/6/24/21301959/netflix-july-2020-orginals-licensed-tv-movies-competitors
3. In 2016, the most recent breakdown available, Netflix produced 11 documentary features and 35 unscripted series. These numbers are up from 2/1 in 2012, 7/6 in 2013, 7/6 in 2014, 7/15 in 2015. Of course "unscripted" series includes both docuseries and reality television, begging the question, as this essay does, where the border between genres lies if indeed a border exists at all. Sam Cook, "50+ Netflix Statistics and Facts that Define the Company's Dominance in 2021," *Comparitech*, May 18, 2021, www.comparitech.com/blog/vpn-privacy/netflix-statistics-facts-figures/

   As Disney and HBO entered the streaming market in 2020–21, it was clear Netflix was not just their primary competitor, but the overwhelming leader in the streaming market. This applies to all genres, not only nonfiction. Natalie Jarvey, "The High Cost of Chasing Netflix," *The Hollywood Reporter*, February 3, 2021, www.hollywoodreporter.com/business/business-news/the-high-cost-of-chasing-netflix-4126576/
4. Sudeep Sharma, "Netflix and the Documentary Boom," in *The Netflix Effect: Technology and Entertainment in the 21st Century*, eds. Kevin McDonald and Daniel Smith Rowsey, (New York: Bloomsbury, 2016), 143.
5. In addition to sheer volume, "[S]ince 2016, Netflix Docs Have Won an Oscar Ever Year, With Wins for *American Factory, Period: End of Sentence, Icarus* and *The White Helmets*," *Goldberg*, 2021, n.p.

6. Mike Snider, "Netflix, Amazon Prime, Disney+ and Hulu Are Stream-ing Favorites as Americans Subscribe to More Services Amid Covid 19," *USA Today*, February 16, 2021, www.usatoday.com/story/tech/2021/02/16/netflix-amazon-streaming-video-disney-hulu-hbo-max-peacock/6759020002/

7. Denise Petski, "*Tiger King* Draws 34 Million Viewers in First 10 Days on Netflix, Eclipsing *Stranger Things*," Deadline.com, April 8, 2020, https://deadline.com/2020/04/tiger-king-34-million-viewers-first-10-days-stranger-thi-ngs-2-1202903556/

8. Cynthia Littleton, "Netflix: *Tiger King* Watched by 64 Million Households, *Love Is Blind* Grabs 30 Million," *Variety.com*, April 21, 2020, https://variety.com/2020/tv/news/netflix-tiger-king-love-is-blind-viewing-64-million-1234586272/

9. Netflix, "What We Watched This Year: The Stories That Helped Us Escape at Home," Press Release, December 10, 2020, https://about.netflix.com/en/news/what-we-watched-2020-on-netflix

10. Lauren Berlant, *Cruel Optimism* (Durham, NC: Duke University Press, 2011), 6.

11. Jason Mittell, "A Cultural Approach to Television Genre Theory," *Cinema Journal* 40, no. 3 (Spring 2001): 3.

12. Netflix, "*Tiger King: Murder Mayhem and Madness:* Series Information," *Netflix.com*, March 20, 2020.

13. Tanya Horeck, *Justice on Demand: True Crime in the Digital Streaming Era* (Detroit, MI: Wayne State University Press, 2019).

14. Ron Simon, "The Changing Definition of Reality Television," in *Thinking Outside the Box: A Contemporary Television Genre Reader*, eds. Gary R. Edg-erton and Brain G. Rose (Lexington, KY: The University Press of Kentucky, 2008), 188.

15. Ibid., 194.

16. Bill Nichols, *Introduction to Documentary* (Bloomington, IN: Indiana Univer-sity Press, 2001), 39.

17. Mareike Jenner, *Netflix & the Re-invention of Television* (Cham, Switzerland: Palgrave Macmillan, 2018), 109–38.

18. Joe Flint, "Meet the Woman Who Made Netflix's *Tiger King* Must-See Quaran-tine TV," *Washington Post*, May10, 2020, Online, https://on.wsj.com/3mlJf0m

19. We capitalize White and Whiteness throughout our work in order to make it clear that White is a racial category, not a norm against which other racial cat-egories are differentiated, as a lower case w may imply. We follow the 2020 decision of the *Washington Post* to change their style guide in this respect in the wake of a year of near-continual anti-racist protests across the United States.

20. Ben Travers, "*Making a Murderer* Review: Part 2 Is a Long, Painful Look at Old Evidence With Little New to Say," *Indiewire.com*, October 19, 2018, www.indiewire.com/2018/10/making-a-murderer-season-2-review-netflix-spoilers-1202012937/

   "*Making a Murder* Season 2 Is Too Long (and Nothing Happens)," *Screenrant. com*, n.d., https://screenrant.com/making-murderer-season-2-mistake-netflix-steven-avery/2/; Sonya Saraiya, "Review: *Making a Murderer* Season 2 Can't Make a Case for Itself," *Vanity Fair*, October 19, 2018, www.vanityfair. com/hollywood/2018/10/making-a-murderer-part-2-season-2-review-netflix; Paul Tassi, "Nobody Likes Netflix's New *Tiger King* Episode," *Forbes.com*, April 13, 2020, www.forbes.com/sites/paultassi/2020/04/13/nobody-likes-netflixs-new-tiger-king-episode/?sh=4f645bebb28d

21. Reality TV experienced a boom during this strike because the editors who crafted story lines were not classed as writers and were not part of the WGA. As a result, reality TV was able to maintain production and fill huge gaps in TV schedules while fictional programs were halted by the labor conflict.
22. *The Hollywood Reporter* Staff, " 'Tiger King' Editor Reveals How the "Bonkers" Story Unfolded in the Cutting Room," *Behind the Screen Podcast*, Episode 61 (April 6, 2020), www.hollywoodreporter.com/behind-screen/tiger-king-editor-how-bonkers-story-unfolded-cutting-room-1288542
23. John Corner, "Civic Visions: Forms of Documentary," in *Television: The Critical View*, sixth edition, ed. Horace Newcomb (Oxford: Oxford University Press, 2000), 207–36.
24. Wenlei Ma, "Netflix's Lisa Nishimura, the Woman Behind Tiger King and Making a Murderer, on How She Finds Hit Movies and TV Shows," *News.com.au*, July 18, 2020, www.news.com.au/technology/home-entertainment/tv/netflixs-lisa-nishimura-the-woman-behind-tiger-king-and-making-a-murderer-on-how-she-finds-hit-movies-and-tv-shows/news-story/d194e963302520265c589155a4758c96
25. Lynne Joyrich, "Reality TV Trumps Politics," *The Contemporary Condition*, November 2016, Online, http://contemporarycondition.blogspot.com/2016/11/reality-tv-trumps-politics.html
26. For discussions of the cult of Trump, see David Paleologos, "A 'Cult President'? Breaking Down Trump's Support," *USA Today,* December 24, 2020, Online; Joe Hagen, " 'So Many Great, Educated, Functional People Were Brainwashed': Can Trump's Cult of Followers Be Deprogrammed?" *Vanity Fair*, January 21, 2021, Online; Jill Tucker, "Experts See Cult-Like Behavior in Trump's Most Extreme Followers: Breaking Them Free May Not Be Easy," *The San Francisco Chronicle*, January 17, 2021, Online.
27. Horeck, *Justice on Demand*, 147.
28. Linda Williams, "Film Bodies: Gender, Genre, and Excess," *Film Quarterly* 44, no. 4 (Summer, 1991): 2–13.
29. Karin Bruillard, "How *Tiger King* Became a Tale More About People Than Big Cats," *Washington Post*, April 6, 2020, Online, www.washingtonpost.com/science/2020/04/06/tiger-king-joe-exotic/
30. Brett Mills, *The Sitcom* (Edinburgh: Edinburgh University Press, 2009); Taylor Nygaard and Jorie Lagerwey, *Horrible White People* (New York: New York University Press), 75–114.
31. Horeck, *Justice on Demand*, 147. Citing Geoff King, " 'Killingly Funny': Mixing Modalities in New Hollywood's Comedy-With-Violence," in *New Hollywood Violence*, ed. Stephen Jay Schneider (Manchester: Manchester University Press, 2004), 130.
32. Jorie Lagerwey and Taylor Nygaard, "*Tiger King*'s Meme-ification of White Grievance and the Normalization of Misogyny," *Forum: Tiger King. Communication, Culture and Critique* 13, no. 4 (December 2020): 560–3.
33. Julie Lim, "*Tiger King* Is the Flamin' Hot Cheetos of Netflix, in the Best and Worst Ways," *The Daily Californian*, April 22, 2020, Online, www.dailycal.org/2020/04/22/tiger-king-is-the-flamin-hot-cheetos-of-netflix-in-the-best-and-worst-ways/. See also Sophie Gilbert, "The Most-Watched Show in America Is a Moral Failure," *The Atlantic*, April 7, 2020, Online, www.theatlantic.com/culture/archive/2020/04/netflix-tiger-king-is-an-ethical-trainwreck/609568/; Andrew Paredes, "Review: Watching Netflix's 'Tiger King'

Is Like Watching a Car Crash Into an Oil Tanker," *ABS-CBN News*, March 31, 2020, Online, https://news.abs-cbn.com/ancx/culture/movies/03/31/20/review-watching-netflixs-tiger-king-is-like-watching-a-car-crash-into-an-oil-tanker; Lila Peachy, "Why Is Tiger King the Train Wreck We Can't Stop Watching?" *The Articulator*, April 12, 2020, Online, https://medium.com/articulator/why-is-tiger-king-the-train-wreck-we-cannot-stop-watching-4834a3f1e23f

34. Sophie Gilbert, "The Most-Watched Show in America Is a Moral Failure," *The Atlantic*, April 7, 2020, Online, www.theatlantic.com/culture/archive/2020/04/netflix-tiger-king-is-an-ethical-trainwreck/609568/

35. Hollis Griffin, "Living Through It: Anger, Laughter, and Internet Memes in Dark Times," *International Journal of Cultural Studies* 24, no. 3 (2021): 381–97.

36. Judith Hall, "The U.S. Has an Empathy Deficit," *Scientific American*, September 17, 2020, Online, www.scientificamerican.com/article/the-us-has-an-empathy-deficit/

37. Terri E. Givens, *Radical Empathy: Finding a Path to Bridging Racial Divides* (Bristol, UK: Policy Press, 2021).

38. Brené Brown, "RSA Short: Empathy," *BreneBrown.com*, December 10, 2013, https://brenebrown.com/videos/rsa-short-empathy/

39. Leah Anderst, "Calling to Witness: Complicating Autobiography and Narrative Empathy in Marlon Riggs's *Tongues Untied*," *Studies in Documentary Film* 13, no. 1 (2019): 73–89.

40. Tanya Horeck, "'A Film That Will Rock You to Your Core': Emotion and Affect in *Dear Zachary* and the Real Crime Documentary," *Crime Media Culture* (2014): 1–17.

41. Leah Anderst, "Calling to Witness: Complicating Autobiography and Narrative Empathy in Marlon Riggs's *Tongues Untied*," *Studies in Documentary Film* 13, no. 1 (2019): 75. Citing Sara Ahmed, *The Cultural Politics of Emotion* (New York: Routledge, 2004), 30.

42. Lisa Nakamura, "Feeling Good About Feeling Bad: Virtuous Virtual Reality and the Automation of Racial Empathy," *Journal of Visual Culture* 19, no. 1 (2020).

43. Ibid.

44. Laura Grindstaff and Susan Murry, "Reality Celebrity: Branded Affect and the Emotion Economy," *Public Culture* 27, no. 1 (2015): 109–35. doi:10.1215/08992363–2798367

45. Horace Newcomb and Paul M. Hirsch, "Television as Cultural Forum," *Quarterly Review of Film Studies* 8 (Summer 1983): 45–55.

46. Taylor Nygaard and Jorie Lagerwey, *Horrible White People: Gender, Genre, and Television's Precarious Whiteness* (New York: New York University Press, 2020).

47. Benedict Anderson posits the idea of nation coming not from geographical bounds, but from shared cultural experiences. The imagined community of television viewers is the public created by a major hit TV show and, in many cases, the collective experience of watching with social media (see Horeck in this volume for more on *Tiger King*'s social media presence). While the two communities are not necessarily identical, it is also the public imagined and targeted by programmers and advertisers. For example, Nygaard and Lagerwey have posited class-based taste cultures as an example of a border-crossing imagined community that is both actual viewing public and target market

for streaming content providers. Benedict Anderson, *Imagined Communities: Reflections on the Origin and Spread of Nationalism* (New York: Verso Books, 1991). Taylor Nygaard and Jorie Lagerwey, *Horrible White People: Gender, Genre, and Television's Precarious Whiteness* (New York: New York University Press, 2020).

48. Ramon Lobato, "Rethinking International TV Flows Research in the Age of Netflix," *Television and New Media* (2017): 12, Online First, doi:10.1177/1527476417708245

3 #carolebaskinkilledherhusband

The gender politics of *Tiger King* meme culture

Tanya Horeck

To begin to account for the wild popularity and spreadability of *Tiger King* as a documentary text, allow me to share two related anecdotes: the first occurred one morning in September 2020 when I overheard my nine-year-old son (who had never seen or even heard of *Tiger King*) cheerfully singing to himself as he got ready for school about how Carole Baskin murdered her husband and fed his dead body to tigers: "Carole Baskin. Killed her, husband, whacked him. Can't convince me that it didn't happen. Fed him to tigers, they snackin'. What's happenin'? Carole Baskin."[1] The second took place a few weeks later, as I prepared to teach *Tiger King* to my undergraduate documentary film students in the United Kingdom. My son walked into my room, glanced at my laptop screen, and said with surprise and interest: "Is that really Carole Baskin – the woman who killed her husband and fed him to tigers?"

Out of the mouths of babes this is, in essence, the key cultural takeaway from Netflix's streaming docuseries, *Tiger King: Murder, Mayhem and Madness*: that Carole Baskin, the owner-operator of Big Cat Rescue sanctuary in Hillsborough County, Florida, killed her second husband, the millionaire Don Lewis, and fed him to tigers. That there is no evidence – in the documentary or elsewhere – to substantiate these claims is largely inconsequential to the legions of people worldwide who participated in the *Tiger King* TikTok dance craze. The trend was created by TikTok user Caleb Jaxin, who, on April 5, 2020, uploaded a video of himself dressed as *Tiger King* star "Joe Exotic," performing a 15-second *Tiger King* parody to the dance moves of the rapper Megan Thee Stallion's #Savagedancechallenge.[2] Since then, the Carole Baskin song and dance has been repeated in millions of TikTok videos. As with other TikTok crazes, the Carole Baskin/*Tiger King* trend is an ear worm remix, lip-sync, and social dance that consists of hypnotic "little loops of codified gesture."[3] The cosplay aspect of the craze, in which people of all ages (including very young children and in some cases babies) dressed up as Joe Exotic and/or Carole Baskin – wearing

DOI: 10.4324/9781003157205-4

baseball caps with painted mustaches and goatees on their faces, sporting eyebrow rings, bleached mullets, and/or long blonde wigs with flower garlands around their heads while attired in head to toe leopard print – was also central to the performative pleasures of the trend.

The dance craze is a central part of the now deeply entrenched internet folklore around *Tiger King*, with the remix lyrics functioning as a modern-day murder ballad – only one in which the woman is the aggressor, not the victim.[4] Indeed, the TikTok trend assumed and insisted upon Carole Baskin's status as a murderess with some considerable glee, as did the thousands of other *Tiger King* memes that circulated across social media platforms after the docuseries' full drop release on Netflix. To give some perspective on the viewer/user engagement with the series: according to the Nielsen ratings, *Tiger King* was watched by 34.3 million unique viewers in its first 10 days of release in the United States. At the time of writing, the hashtag #carolebaskinkilledherhusband has had 36.6 million views on TikTok.

In this essay, I unpack the cultural logics of *Tiger King* memes in order to consider what they have to reveal about the affective investment in the streaming-era long-form true crime documentary and its often-troublesome gender politics. Asaf Nissenbaum and Limor Shifman define memes as: "groups of digital items (such as images or videos) that share common characteristics, are created with awareness of each other, and are distributed online by multiple participants."[5] Though memes predate the internet, they flourish in an online participatory environment where they are able to multiply and spread as humorous, entertaining objects. As internet scholars have demonstrated, the apparent silliness or frivolity of internet memes belies their social functionality and interest as sites for the articulation of deep-rooted cultural ideals and structures of belief.[6] Serving as "conduits of affect on the internet,"[7] memes circulate as expressions of public sentiment and hypercharged bundles of emotive reaction and response. In the case of *Tiger King*, the affective value of the memetic response was heightened considerably by the fact that the series was released during the first phase of lockdown for COVID-19 in March 2020. At a time when people were experiencing social distance, *Tiger King* was received as a blockbuster true crime docuseries that brought people together. The *Tiger King* memes that emerged out of the series formed networked "affective publics"[8] that produced "*feelings* of community" if not necessarily community itself.[9]

What is so compelling about *Tiger King* memes, produced during quarantine for COVID-19, is how they serve as a record of audience response – both to the stranger-than-fiction documentary blockbuster and

Mary
@maryyyyrosee

Me: I can't stop thinking about, talking about, or reading about the coronavirus

Netflix: let me introduce you to Joe Exotic and Carole Baskin. #TigerKing

♡ 6,590 2:39 AM - Mar 23, 2020

💬 2,226 people are talking about this   boredpanda.com

Figure 3.1 Tiger King as a welcome distraction from coronavirus.

to lockdown life in a global health crisis (Figure 3.1). As a true crime scholar, I am fascinated by *Tiger King* memes for what they reveal about the affective power of digital-era true crime as "online TV" or "social television," in which "online content and interactions are as important as (or more important than) the shows being broadcast."[10] In their mocking tone toward the stereotyped "white trash" characters put on display for viewer delectation in *Tiger King*, the memes assume a kind of "gawking viewing position," which is encouraged by the docuseries itself.[11] In so doing, they expose the affective machinery of *Tiger King*'s dubious image ethics and the problematic relation that the documentary assumes to its classed and gendered subjects.

The most popular set of *Tiger King* memes by far are those that mock Carole Baskin and generate humor out of the accusation that she murdered her then-husband Don Lewis in 1997. It is telling that it is not any of the actual crimes and misdemeanors on display in *Tiger King* (crimes which, it should be said, are mainly organized and executed by networks of toxic white men) – from the business of monetizing grubby cub petting and selfie taking, to outright animal abuse and slaughter, to the illegal breeding and trading of baby cubs, and to conspiracy to commit murder-for-hire – that captured the public imagination. Instead, what most captivated viewers is the rumor and salacious speculation regarding an unproven murder from the 1990s for which there is not even a dead body. Feeding into a wider appetite for desktop sleuthing and internet detection, it is, of course, the very mystery surrounding the disappearance of Don Lewis that tantalized the public. However, while it is possible that *some* internet sleuths are keen to help the Hillsborough County Sheriff's Office in Florida in their reinvestigation of Lewis's disappearance, it is also apparent that, in large part, the memetic culture around Carole Baskin evinces no real interest in crime solving. Rather, the pleasure derives from asserting the fact of her guilt as a *fait accompli*; as one media report asserts: "Here's why the internet thinks Carole Baskin killed her husband: Reason One: Because she did."[12]

In truth, it is impossible to say whether or not Carole Baskin "did it," but I argue that part of the series' appeal as ultimate "lockdown viewing" derives from how it actively encourages viewers to revel in the accusation. In its overt and at times quite stylized visual display of its documentary participants as "characters" for viewers to respond to (and judge), *Tiger King* actively fuels a long-standing dispute between Joe Exotic, the star and "Tiger King" of the series, and his nemesis, big cats activist, Carole Baskin. The spread of the storytelling over seven episodes (with a tacky, eighth "pandemic episode" added on) is engineered to encourage binge-watching with viewer attention being carefully managed and directed through the liberal use of devices such as money shots, hooks, and cliffhangers. As I have argued elsewhere, despite its user-directed, "interactive" appearance, true crime in the Netflix era tends to generate affective response and judgment in highly predetermined ways, designed to evoke collective emotional reactions that automate viewers to hit "play next episode."[13]

In its clickbait, play-next-episode approach to documentary filmmaking, *Tiger King* creates the affective conditions for a sympathetic response to Joe Exotic and for the corresponding vilification of Carole Baskin, which is abundantly evidenced in *Tiger King* memes and their accompanying viral hashtags: #carolefuckingbaskin, #thatbitchcarole-baskin, and #carolebaskinkilledherhusband. Joe Exotic's pathological and misogynistic hatred of Baskin, as depicted to exuberant effect in the docuseries, has seeped into networked popular responses and become a central, if problematic and unexamined element, of the "feel-good" vibe surrounding *Tiger King* as the perfect pandemic entertainment. My aim here is to consider the ideological implications of the "mood work"[14] performed by *Tiger King* in its online economies of engagement. As I will demonstrate, the memetic interaction with the docuseries amplifies, and repurposes, the ugly gender tropes that lie at its core. As an embodiment of the affective responses solicited by the series itself, *Tiger King* memes cultivate and ultimately commodify a networked misogyny dressed up as cathartic corona comedy.

Corona comedy

To gain a sense of how viewers respond to *Tiger King*, it is instructive to turn to *Gogglebox*, the TV program that shows ordinary viewers watching topical television shows with their friends and/or family members in the comfort of their homes. Included in the April 13, 2020 episode of the British version of the program,[15] the montage of various *Goggleboxers'* reactions to the first two episodes of *Tiger King* demonstrates the full range of response, from bemusement and amazement ("he's driving with a tiger in his passenger seat?!") to snarky judgment over Joe Exotic ("ooh he's weird!/He's a fucking nutcase"), to gasps of genuine shock and horror over the terrible incident in which Saff, one of the zoo's employees, has his arm bitten off by a tiger ("oh my god!"), to dismay and more judgment ("he's more worried about his fucking money than the poor lass with her arm torn off!"), to blatant mockery of Joe's husband, John Finlay ("where's his teeth?"), and finally to paroxysms of laughter at the end of the second episode as viewers witness the "three ring circus" that is the wedding of Joe to his two (straight) husbands ("look at the state of all three of them!"). The *Gogglebox* montage illustrates the wildly careening reactions solicited by the crash-bam aesthetics of *Tiger King*: from baffled amusement, to superiority and judgment, to shock and horror, to mockery and pleasure in the shared laughter at the nuttiness of it all. That the *Gogglebox* viewers in this case are British only heightens the "us and them" ethnographic thrust of *Tiger King* as a documentary that invites viewers to rubberneck at the lives of cultural others.

In her insightful essay, "The Casual Horror of Boredom in *Tiger King*," Pavithra Prasad argues that hours of "unabated exposure to the turpitude of *Tiger King*'s events, characters, injuries, and deaths mediates a spectatorial narcosis that cannot respond solidly to any one outrage. The cascade of follies is intentional, strategic, and effective in rendering the audience complicit in its carnivalesque horror."[16] Prasad puts her finger on *Tiger King*'s particular form of attention capture, which encourages quick-fire responses to short-form tableaus of weirdness and wickedness as the narrative lurches from one thing to the next. In certain respects, *Tiger King*'s aesthetic calls to mind YouTube and its sorting algorithms in which videos are lined up, one after the other, in a leveling out of distinction that mingles "life and death, laughter and horror indiscriminately."[17] As Prasad argues, shifting between boredom and horror, the "shock and awe" strategies of *Tiger King* induce "a rote and abject chortling at the docuseries' relentless evocation of our capacity to be stunned."[18] By the end, Prasad suggests, we are left numbed and depleted.

Before we turn to the memes, that is. As creative cogs in the affective machinery of the shock and boredom attention economy described by Prasad, *Tiger King* memes offer a temporary but rejuvenating emotional release in their short-form condensation of the docuseries' real-life cast of characters and scenarios into manageable "affective nuggets."[19] The bonding power of *Tiger King* memes demonstrates what Jenny Sundén and Susanna Paasonen call " 'affective homophily,' the love of feeling the same that brings people together through networked expressions of similar feeling."[20] *Tiger King* memes make reference to the shared experiences of pandemic life, with the Netflix series' account of the eccentric machinations, rivalries, and sexual proclivities of zookeepers and big cat animal owners in Oklahoma and Florida being seen as a form of welcome entertainment and distraction during lockdown. The memes self-consciously acknowledge the shared experience of astonishment at the "weirdness" of the series and suggest *Tiger King*'s therapeutic value as a mood enhancer and a way of relieving the boredom of lockdown.

As the coronavirus crisis deepened, and other periods of lockdown had to be endured, *Tiger King* memes were also used as a way of expressing or discharging public emotion at the annus horribilis that was 2020. In one popular meme, the quip "If 2020 was a person" is pasted at the top of an image of the outlandish Joe Exotic with his arm around one of his tigers (Figure 3.2). Other memes extracted images from the documentary in order to crack jokes about the realities of lockdown life. In a widely circulated example, a photograph of Joe Exotic and his two husbands in bed together, shirtless and showing off their tattoos in a sultry pose for the camera, has this as its punchline: "All the boys coming out of self-isolation after cutting their own hair for months #tigerking" (Figure 3.3). The pandemic joke makes reference to the men's out of style haircuts – the "mullets" which

Figure 3.2 Joe Exotic as comical embodiment of a difficult year.

Joe Exotic himself rightly anticipates in an interview in Episode 1 of *Tiger King* as something that would be remarked upon and mocked by middle-class, urbane viewers. One presumes that this photo was originally part of Joe Exotic's collection of private photos of his domestic life with his two young husbands. It is repurposed in the documentary as part of a montage of photographs and video footage demonstrating the less than conventional three-way or "thruple" relationship between the men. The use of the photo in the meme is thus an appropriation of an appropriation; it is what documentary film theorist and co-editor of this collection, Jaimie Baron, refers to as a "misuse in the sense that its new use was not intended or at least not anticipated by its original producer."[21] As Baron demonstrates in her book *Reuse, Misuse, Abuse: The Ethics of Audiovisual Appropriation in the Digital Era*, the ethics of "misusing" or reappropriating preexisting audiovisual

All the boys coming out of self-isolation after cutting their own hair for months. #TigerKing 🐯

Figure 3.3 Extracting images from *Tiger King* to crack jokes about lockdown life.

material is complex, especially when it comes to documentary footage of actual people and events.[22]

Memes, by definition, remix, repurpose, and "misuse" images for the purposes of humor, which is often ironic. *Tiger King* memes are what meme theorists call "image macros," which, as Ryan Milner explains, make "their point by overlaying a quip on a single still image."[23] Generally speaking, *Tiger King* memes can be divided into three categories: (1) Joe Exotic/*Tiger King* pandemic memes, (2) Carole Baskin murdered her husband memes, and (3) That bitch Carole Baskin/Goddamn Carole Baskin memes. There is considerable overlap between these three categories. So, for example, many of the "That bitch Carole Baskin/Goddamn Carole Baskin" memes make a joke (à la Joe Exotic) of blaming Carole Baskin for COVID-19 and are therefore also pandemic memes.

In their account of internet humor, Sundén and Paasonen note that "Theories of humor tend to be divided into three classic types: incongruity, relief and superiority."[24] *Tiger King* memes fall into all three of these categories: they function through incongruity by using the "crazy" lifestyles and internecine disputes of big cat owners as a way of ironically commenting on the hum drum mundanities of lockdown life; they use humor "as a social pressure valve of sorts" and a means of venting and destressing in the midst of a global health crisis; and they generate superior laughter that "establish(es) and maintain(s) social hierarchies by laughing at something or someone,"[25] namely women, stereotyped "white trash,"[26] and queer others.

"A laugh," as Sundén and Paasonen note, is "not necessarily happy," but it is always a means of "affective expression" and "active release," which can hold a range of negative affects including "anxiety, sadness and anger."[27] The use of laughter as a "vehicle for contempt"[28] is on display throughout *Tiger King*, as well as in many of the memes produced in response to it. To fully understand the memetic culture that sprung up around *Tiger King*, it is necessary to examine how the documentary series itself establishes fertile conditions for contemptuous networked laughter and for loving to hate Carole Baskin.

The *Tiger King* show

If the true crime documentary blockbuster has become a sure and steady staple of Netflix's original offering since the release of *Making a Murderer* in 2015, then *Tiger King* arguably represents the "decadent" stage of the subgenre, the point at which its conventions become fully baroque and parodic. It is revealing in regard to the latter that when discussing *Tiger King* and his fascination with the eccentricities of animal people, director and animal conservationist Eric Goode has cited Christopher Guest's mockumentary *Best in Show* (2000) as an influence.[29] Goode's personal delight as a documentarian in capturing the sheer oddness of his subjects is palpable throughout *Tiger King*, as when he persuades Joe Exotic to keep his baseball hat off in an interview to show off his bleached blonde mullet ("I like it! I like it!" he reassures him) or when he arrives at the Big Cat Rescue sanctuary to interview Carole Baskin and notes to his companion (assumed to be co-director Rebecca Chaiklin) with delight: "oh she's dressed perfectly." Throughout all seven episodes, Joe's husband John Finlay is interviewed without his shirt on (the directors claim this is because he wanted to show off his tattoos, while Finlay himself says that he was strongly encouraged to go shirtless).[30]

It is symptomatic of the overwhelming impact of the sensational content of the documentary that it is quite easy to forget the extent to which Goode, one half of the documentary filmmaking team with Rebecca Chaiklin, features in the documentary. Yet, subsequent viewings reveal him to be a significant physical presence in *Tiger King*; his asides to camera and his prompts to the various interviewees play a significant role in mediating viewer responses to the material.[31]

If Goode guides viewer response through his reserved bemusement at his documentary subjects, so, too, do Joe Exotic's bombastic performances of hatred in his vignettes on Carole Baskin for his internet show, which form a reality spectacle within a reality spectacle in *Tiger King*. In this "found footage," Joe and his cronies defile blow-up doll facsimiles of Carole, read excerpts aloud from what is allegedly her private diaries, and stage elaborate and violent scenes of misogynist ridicule. Just as Joe Exotic invited his internet followers to laugh at these segments, *Tiger King* as a documentary encourages laughter at Joe's reality vignettes through its framing of them as part of the "crazy" story it is telling. As Taylor Nygaard and Jorie Lagerwey, my fellow contributors to this volume, note in their perceptive reading of *Tiger King's* "meme-ification," *Tiger King* presents white male grievance and anger as "comedic spectacle" and sanctions it by "rendering it laughable."[32]

Tiger King also invites laughter at its own constructed reality tableaus, through intercutting interview footage with more stylized shots of its documentary subjects. For example, in Episode 1, "Not Your Average Joe," a montage of interviews with the white male big cat owners, Doc Antle and Joe Exotic, in which they express their hatred and antipathy for Carole Baskin, is juxtaposed with images, presented in slow motion, of Baskin walking, her long blonde hair flowing behind her. This editing and slow-motion presentation has the effect of fixing Baskin (described by her husband Howard as the "Mother Teresa of cats") as an object of comedic derision, and it is repeated throughout the docuseries. Joe Exotic might come in for similar comedic treatment at times, with stylized close-up shots of him facing the camera directly, but the documentary's affective energies are more firmly aligned with him.[33]

Tiger King's tendency toward generating a certain campy amusement at the story it is telling grows darker when it is aimed at Baskin. Consider, for example, Episode 3, "The Secret," which is arguably the "hooked episode" of *Tiger King*, when viewers become committed to watching the entire series through to the end.[34] The episode sets up a true crime mystery around the disappearance of Don Lewis, which is punctuated by strategically placed close-up images of tigers growling and footage of Joe Exotic's "Here Kitty Kitty" music video, which features a look alike Carole laughing and feeding dead body parts to her big cats. Joe Exotic's assertion that Don Lewis's family demanded the police DNA test the meat grinder on

Carole's property is accompanied by recreated footage of a meat grinder churning out ground meat – an image which is repeated a second time, for comic effect, when Carole refutes the meat grinding assertion. The episode ends with Eric Goode pointedly asking Don Lewis' first wife and adult children if they are afraid of Carole Baskin. When first wife Gladys Lewis responds in the affirmative, the documentary includes a close-up, stylized image of Carole Baskin looking straight into the camera, which has the effect of making her look villainous. This is juxtaposed with a close-up of Joe Exotic also looking straight to camera, overlaid by an audio clip of him saying: "I'm taking Carole on because everyone else is scared to. She has a lot of answering to do. Her day's coming." The episode ends here, enticing viewers to keep (binge-)watching to find out if Carole will indeed get her comeuppance. It's a GIF-able conclusion that calls to mind a common structured reality television setup, in which personalities are pitted against one another to generate maximum conflict, and to prompt extensive social media response from viewers.

Yet, the familiar structure here serves to disguise rather than critique the persistent mistreatment not only of animals but also of people on display in the series. Buried beneath *Tiger King*'s constant barrage of campy images and lurid reality TV style discord are disturbing stories of sexual exploitation and abuse. Both Doc Antle and Joe Exotic are arguably shown to exploit and manipulate young people – young women in the case of Doc Antle and young men in the case of Joe Exotic – for their sexual gratification. The docuseries shows Doc Antle introducing his various wives as though they were animals at his park – that's "Rajnee, the little Italian lady," "there is Moksha, the pretty blonde with the big teeth and the bright, big smile." There are no interviews with the women themselves. Even the interview with Barbara Fisher, a former employee of Doc's, which is apparently in the documentary to offer balance and a counter perspective, is, to an extent, played for laughs, as her account of poor working conditions is comically contrasted with Doc's claim that his animal park is "Shangri-La."

Joe Exotic's relationship with his two young husbands is also presented through a comedic tone. From the start, Exotic's gayness is presented as something that contributes to his eccentricity – not only by Exotic himself, who is hugely self-conscious of his public image and how he presents as unconventional – but also by the documentary which merrily introduces him through one of its talking heads, "as a completely insane, gay, gun-toting, drug-addict fanatic." The information that his husbands, John Finlay and Travis Maldonado, are straight and are there for the meth Exotic supplies them with is something that is withheld from viewers and presented as a plot twist (or punchline) in later episodes. *Tiger King* introduces Travis through found video footage in which he gazes into a camera, looking vulnerable and drugged up, as Exotic coaches him to say he is called Travis Maldonado. The use of this footage constitutes, for me, one of the most disturbing "misuses" of found footage in the docuseries. What makes it disturbing is the plaintive way in which a young Travis looks to the camera (and to us) and the cavalier way in which the documentary flits away from his look as it moves on to other topics.[35] Ultimately, Travis's suicide is rather reprehensibly withheld from viewers in the service of being a plot revelation. In Episode 5, his death is finally revealed and, although the video footage of Travis shooting himself is not shown, the documentary includes surveillance footage of Joe Exotic's campaign manager, Joshua Dial's, shocked, open-mouthed reaction to the horrific incident.

There are other horrors that get buried by the *Tiger King* show. In Episode 3, Carole Baskin reports how, when she was 14 years old, she was raped at gunpoint by three men. Her fundamentalist Christian family blamed her for the gang rape and she left home at 15. By 17, she was married and had a baby. Her husband was abusive, and she eventually left him in her early twenties for Don Lewis who, by all accounts, was a controlling womanizer. Excerpts from Carole Baskin's diary testify to her abusive experience with Don. *Tiger King* shows Joe Exotic reading aloud excerpts from Baskin's ostensible diary in a mocking, accusatory tone: "I wish there was some way out for me." Joe then turns to camera, "I'd say she found a way out, wouldn't you?" alluding to the alleged murder of Don Lewis which Episode 3 probes through interviews, archival footage, and reenactments.

In my analysis of popular true crime blockbusters such as *Serial* (Sarah Koenig, 2014–), *The Jinx: The Life and Deaths of Robert Durst* (Andrew Jarecki, HBO, 2015) and *Making a Murderer* (Laura Ricciardi and Moira Demos, Netflix, 2015), I have noted their tendency to sideline the female victims of male violence. These long-form true crime blockbusters refer to narratives of domestic abuse (and indeed often quote from the diaries of the dead female victims in this regard), but they do not explore them.[36] This mirrors a tendency in popular fictional US serial television such as *The Sopranos* (David Chase, HBO, 1999–2007), *Breaking Bad* (Vince Gilligan, AMC, 2008–2013), and *Game of Thrones* (David Benioff and D.B. Weiss, HBO, 2011–2019) to marginalize "narratives of abuse at the expense of an overwhelming emphasis on the problems of hegemonic masculinity."[37] Of all the theories that *Tiger King* floats for why Carole Baskin allegedly might have killed Don Lewis, it is noteworthy that it never spends time seriously considering the issue of domestic violence. My point, however, is not to introduce a new theory, or more speculation around the alleged murder of Don Lewis, but to reflect on what gets extracted for memes from the documentary and what does not, and how this relates to the popular and normalized misogyny that has become embedded around *Tiger King*.[38]

Strip away the extraneities and subplots and *Tiger King* is, at its essence, a male antihero story. As defined by television theorist Jason Mittell, recent complex serial television is characterized by the rise of the antihero, defined as "unsympathetic, morally questionable, or villainous figures, nearly always male."[39] Serial television and its "long time frame" demands that our interaction with these male antiheroes will "last quite a while."[40] One of the main side effects of male antihero drama, according to TV critic Alan Sepinwall, is that "characters who on paper should be the sympathetic ones become hated by viewers for opposing the protagonist."[41] In the case of *Breaking Bad*, for example, one of the consequences of spending a lot of time with the morally bankrupt and monstrous Walter White was that many viewers grew to loathe his fictional wife, Skyler. The levels of misogynist vitriol were such that actress Anna Gunn, who played Skyler, took out a *New York Times* Op Ed to address the audience response, which included threats against her life. Against a reading of these angry responses to Skyler as random misogyny, Mittell argues that, "Hating Skyler is a significant part of *Breaking Bad's* cultural circulation and thus an aspect of its gender politics as articulated, if not textually intended or justified."[42]

As a documentary with a time frame of 5 hours and 17 minutes, *Tiger King* invites audiences to position themselves with Joe Exotic as an anti-hero figure across its long duration. Joe Exotic is, as many commentators have noted, a figure with Trumpian overtones, presenting himself as a truth-telling straight shooter who cuts through the layers of perceived Carole Baskian hypocrisy. This is, in essence, the gist of the memes and their collective assumption of a Joe Exotic-like position in relation to Carole Baskin, who is cast as a hypocritical figure to be ridiculed. But if the general antipathy toward Carole Baskin is rooted in the audience's investment in Exotic as an antihero and a poor man's Trump – a "plain-talkin' red-blooded American who cuts the crap"[43] – then it is important to note that other *Tiger King* characters are not singled out for similar opprobrium. Indeed, there are other prominent characters in *Tiger King* who "oppose the protagonist," including, most memorably, the figure of Jeff Lowe, who first appears in Episode 4, "Playing with Fire," as an investor who initially tries to help Joe Exotic out of his financial trouble before becoming his enemy for the rest of the series (and beyond). In a show that is replete with displays of toxic masculinity, Jeff Lowe is arguably presented as the most toxic of them all in his casual, hateful, and totally unfiltered expression of rank misogynist viewpoints. And yet, despite the fact that the latter episodes of the docuseries strongly suggest that it was Lowe who helped to take the hit out on Baskin only to then evade prosecution by helping the State indict Exotic, it is worth noting that there has been little or no expression of audience antipathy toward him. Jeff Lowe memes, in other words, had very little traction or spreadability. This suggests that it is not simply about who opposes or stands in the way of the antihero; more specifically, it is about the *woman* who is seen to impede the antihero's action or progress.

The pleasures of hating Carole

The internet is inundated with "that bitch Carole Baskin" and "Carole fucking Baskin" memes. They are the most contagious examples of the "affective homophily" of *Tiger King* as a text that bonds audiences through networked affect.[44] Most typically, the memes consist of an extracted image of Joe Exotic, with the setup to the joke printed at the top and the punchline of "that bitch Carole Baskin" or "Carole Fucking Baskin" appearing at the bottom. The affective force of the gag comes from assigning blame to Carole Baskin as a catch-all figure for both minor and major annoyances, from domestic squabbles over missing Doritos to the quarantine brought about by a global health crisis (Figure 3.4).

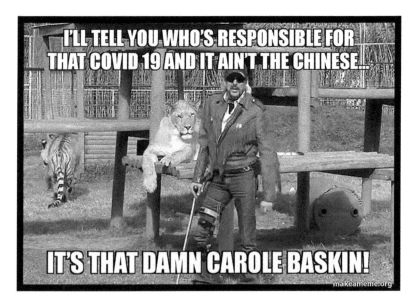

Figure 3.4 Carole Baskin as a catch-all blame figure.

What is being extracted from *Tiger King* are not only images but, more significantly, affective energies or intensities, which invite users to assume the position of an aggrieved white man. Regardless of the particular ways in which they are framed, Carole Baskin memes are prevalent examples of what Sarah Banet-Weiser refers to as "networked popular misogyny," which spreads through rapid online communication and which often relies "upon the idea that men have been *injured* by women" in the sense that they have somehow been "denied rights."[45]

But beyond the rather basic online sexist humor of the memes themselves, what is fascinating to analyze is the force of their affective charge as they travel across social media sites and become further unmoored from the specificities of the docuseries and its cluster of themes around animal abuse, toxic masculinity, and the big cat captivity market in the United States. Summoning up an affective mood of joviality, Carole Baskin memes build a carnivalesque atmosphere around the ridicule of middle-aged white femininity.[46] Baskin is mocked as the "cat lady" of "cat ladies," a specific object of gendered derision in society. As caricatures, the memes create a licensed space for misogynist mockery with "that bitch Carole Baskin" emerging as a lockdown catch phrase and a form of cultural venting during quarantine.

Contextually speaking, it should give serious pause that the culture of Carole Baskin memes, which present the idea of female violence as a source of mockery, rose to prominence at the same moment that widespread concerns emerged about gendered domestic abuse during quarantine. As Amanda Taub wrote in a *New York Times* report on April 6, 2020, "Mounting data suggests that domestic abuse is acting like an opportunistic infection, flourishing in the conditions created by the pandemic."[47] With reports of a spike in calls to domestic abuse hotlines, the United Nations urged governments "to put women's safety first as they respond to the pandemic."[48] Though Carole Baskin memes do not openly dialogue with these reports or with concerns over domestic violence against women, it is nonetheless significant that they should emerge at the same time and that they should serve as an outlet for the expression of public emotion over the conditions of lockdown. Even if in jest, memes such as "Marked Safe From That Bitch Carole Baskin Today" exhibit hostility toward women and are part of a wider social media climate of gendered hate and online misogyny.[49]

The abiding pleasure of Carole Baskin memes appears to derive from their assertion of certitude in her guilt. As Nissenbaum and Shifman have argued, memes are defined not just by their content but on the "stance" that they invite people to assume in relation to that content.[50] In the case

Three things are certain in life:
1. Death
2. Taxes
3. Carole definitely fed her husband to a tiger

Figure 3.5 Carole Baskin memes declare her to be "guilty."

of Carole Baskin memes, individuals are invited to take a firm stance and declare her as "guilty." As noted in one widely circulated meme: "Three things are certain in life: 1. Death 2. Taxes 3. Carole definitely fed her husband to a tiger" (Figure 3.5). In other words, Carole Baskin is guilty because the memes say it is so and there is an affective mood of spirited delight attached to the memetic conjuring forth of a cartoonish female violence, which is accordingly contained and controlled through the very gesture of derision. I find it striking that Carole Baskin memes perpetuate the online misogynistic work begun by Joe Exotic himself who, as recounted in some detail in the docuseries, largely conducted his campaign of hate against Baskin through social media platforms such as Facebook, which he used, in addition to his live internet show, to defame Baskin's character and to humiliate and shame her through misogynist and egregious displays of mockery, sexual violence, and defilement. In a further example of technologically facilitated violence, Exotic and his network of male enablers used Google Earth to stalk Baskin and track the location of her house, allegedly to have her killed while she was riding her bike on her property. Joe Exotic might now be in prison, and without access to Google, Facebook, and Twitter, but the internet abuse of Carole Baskin continues in the form of a networked popular misogyny that is no less insidious for its apparent lightheartedness.

The commodification of *Tiger King*

The extent to which misogynist venting against Carole Baskin has become permissible and popularized is evident in the extraordinary online trade in "that bitch Carole Baskin" commodities, ranging from coffee mugs, t-shirts, and facemasks to birthday cards, Christmas cards, Halloween costumes, and even mini-figurines on sites such as Amazon and Etsy. Much of the *Tiger King* merchandise also references Joe Exotic (and not always solely in relation to Carole Baskin), but in general, the goods are a comical endorsement of his incendiary statements against Baskin. It is unusual for a documentary to be as lucrative a commercial enterprise as this, and the extent of the "merch" indicates the exceptionality of *Tiger King* as a blockbuster event during quarantine for COVID-19. The economic market for true crime is, however, also a logical outcome of the calculated Netflix spectacularization of the genre as a multimedia entertainment and consumer "experience." What is being purchased when one buys *Tiger King* merchandise is a wink and a laugh over shared cultural capital and audience participation in event television. The misogyny emblazoned across the majority of *Tiger King* merchandise is so normalized that one can drink coffee out of one's "Good morning to everyone except that bitch Carole Baskin mug" and blithely see the message on the mug not as evidence of the pervasiveness of structural sexism or misogyny but as an anomalous citation attributed to Joe Exotic as a larger-than-life antihero.[51]

As I have suggested in this essay, the "mayhem" and "madness" of *Tiger King* does not stop with the series itself but is played out across a broader online economy through the sharing of memes and video clips, as well as the selling of merchandise.[52] In addition to being a communal distraction during lockdown, Netflix's *Tiger King* is also a mood and an aesthetic. Whether it is transmitted through O.J. Simpson's one-minute Twitter video, watched by 1.9 million people, in which he pauses his golf game to chuckle about *Tiger King* and how he is certain that Carole Baskin made "tiger sashimi" of Don Lewis, or through Carole Baskin's dismal samba dance to *The Lion King*'s "Circle of Life" on *Dancing with the Stars*, or through her Cameo videos in which she is paid to wish random strangers happy birthday, or through the vogue for people to dress up in their best leopard print fashion using the hashtags #carolebaskin or #tigerking, there is an overwhelming sense of the affective spread and reach of *Tiger King* as a digital media object and site of cultural carnival and performance.

Tiger King memes (like the docuseries itself) tend to be "representationally conservative" in so far as they "reinforce hegemonic patterns" in which women and classed others are mocked and marginalized.[53] However, as digital media theorists have shown, memes and meme culture also hold the potential to tie laughter to more progressive political purposes. To return (briefly) to the TikTok videos mentioned at the start of this essay, it is interesting to think about how these short-form videos latch onto the coordinates of the true crime fantasy at the heart of *Tiger King* and use it as an opportunity for performative repurposing. Though it is beyond the scope of this essay to explore, there is something compelling in the gender fluidity of the Carole Baskin dance craze, with (some) men dressing up as Carole Baskin and (some) women dressing up as Joe Exotic, thus possibly complicating the more conservative stance of a number of *Tiger King* memes.

That memes are far more culturally significant than their frivolous appearance might suggest seems clear; what remains to be seen is whether, and in what ways, they can be deployed in the service of a documentary commitment to social change, particularly when hitched to long-form true crime, which, in its current incarnation, continues to evince a problematic attachment to staging lurid entertainments around questions of guilt and innocence.

Notes

1. Lyrics to the TikTok Tiger King remix of Megan Thee Stallion's "Savage."
2. Gil Kaufman, "Someone Mashed Up "Tiger King" & #SavageChallenge, and It's Megan Thee Stallion-Approved," *Billboard*, April 6, 2020, www.billboard.com/articles/columns/hip-hop/9352281/tiger-king-savagechallenge-mashup-megan-thee-stallion/
3. Wayne Marshall, "Social Dance in the Age of (Anti-) Social Media: Fortnite, Online Video and the Jook at a Virtual Crossroads," *Journal of Popular Music Studies* 3, no. 4 (2019): 3.
4. Murder ballads typically feature women in the role of victims. For a fascinating account of the murder ballad in the bluegrass tradition and its tendency to normalize and excuse violence against women, see Miriam Jones, "Why Do We Love to Sing Murder Ballads? Tradition, Feminism and Bluegrass," *Overland*, November 8, 2017, https://overland.org.au/2017/11/why-do-we-love-to-sing-murder-ballads-tradition-feminism-and-bluegrass/
5. Asaf Nissenbaum and Limor Shifman, "Internet Memes as Contested Cultural Capital: The Case of 4chan's /b/ Board," *New Media & Society* 19, no. 4 (2017): 484.

6. Limor Shifman, *Memes in Digital Culture* (Cambridge, MA: Massachusetts Institute of Technology Press, 2013), 15.

7. Griffin, Hollis, "Living Through It: Anger, Laughter, and Internet Memes in Dark Times," *International Journal of Cultural Studies* 24, no. 3 (2021): 4.

8. Zizi Papacharissi, *Affective Publics: Sentiment, Technology, and Politics* (Oxford: Oxford University Press, 2015).

9. Jodi Dean, "Affective Networks," *Media Tropes eJournal* 2, no. 2 (2010): 22.

10. Donatella Selva, "Social Television: Audience and Political Engagement," *Television & New Media* 17, no. 2 (2016): 161.

11. Taylor Nygaard and Jorie Lagerwey, "Tiger King's Meme-ification of White Grievance and the Normalization of Misogyny," *Communication, Culture & Critique* (2020): 1, doi:10.1093/ccc/tcaa028

12. Bethany Wade, "Here's Why the Internet Thinks Carole Baskin Killed Her Husband," *Film Daily*, April 23, 2020, https://filmdaily.co/obsessions/true-crime/carole-baskin-don-lewis/

13. Tanya Horeck, *Justice on Demand: True Crime in the Digital Streaming Era* (Detroit, MI: Wayne State University Press, 2019), 128.

14. Joke Hermes and Annette Hill, "Television's Undoing of Social Distance," *European Journal of Cultural Studies* 23, no. 4 (2020): 657.

15. See Jason Stolworthy, "Gogglebox Viewers in Hysterics as Channel 4 Stars Watch *Tiger King*: 'I'm in Absolute Stitches,'" *The Independent*, 11 April 2020, www.independent.co.uk/arts-entertainment/tv/news/gogglebox-tiger-king-watch-channel-4-episode-netflix-jenny-lee-a9460521.html

16. Pavithra Prasad, "The Casual Boredom in *Tiger King*," *Communication, Culture & Critique* 13 (2020): 571–3, doi:10.1093/ccc/tcaa030

17. Tina Kendall, "Affect and the Ethics of Snuff in Extreme Art Cinema," in *Snuff: Real Death and Screen Media*, eds. Neil Jackson, Shaun Kimber, Johnny Walker, and Thomas Joseph Watson (New York: Bloomsbury, 2016), 269.

18. Prasad, "The Casual Boredom in *Tiger King*," 572.

19. Dean, "Affective Networks," 21.

20. Jenny Sundén and Susanna Paasonen, *Who's Laughing Now? Feminist Tactics in Social Media* (Cambridge, MA: Massachusetts Institute of Technology Press, 2020), 15.

21. Jaimie Baron, *Reuse, Misuse, Abuse: The Ethics of Audiovisual Appropriation in the Digital Era* (New Brunswick, NJ: Rutgers University Press, 2021), 8.

22. Ibid.

23. Ryan M. Milner, *The World Made Meme: Public Conversations and Participatory Media* (Cambridge, MA: Massachusetts Institute of Technology Press, 2016), 28.

24. Sundén and Paasonen, *Who's Laughing Now?*, 12.

25. Ibid.

26. See Annalee Newitz and Matt Wray's *White Trash: Race and Class in America* (1997) for an indepth discussion of the white trash stereotype.

27. Sundén and Paasonen, *Who's Laughing Now?*, 13–14.

28. Ibid., 14.

29. Doreen St. Félix, "The Crass Pleasures of 'Tiger King,'" *The New Yorker*, 6 April 2020, www.newyorker.com/magazine/2020/04/13/the-crass-pleasures-of-tiger-king

30. Nicole Drum, "Tiger King: John Finlay Reveals Why He Went Shirtless in the Netflix Series," *comicbook.com*, April 13, 2020, https://comicbook.com/tv-shows/news/tiger-king-john-finlay-shirtless-tattoos-netflix/

31. *Tiger King* can be defined as what Bill Nichols refers to as a "participatory documentary," as it consists heavily of interviews and "emphasizes the interaction between filmmaker and subject." See Nichols, *Introduction to Documentary* (Bloomington and Indianapolis, IN: Indiana University Press, 2001), 34.
32. Nygaard and Lagerwey, "*Tiger King's* Meme-ification," 2.
33. As Jaimie Baron reminded me, this affective alignment with Joe Exotic might not have been as strong for viewers if the documentary had included his racism. The directors apparently chose to excise his "unsettling" racist statements because "they didn't have a context in the story." See Tom Skinner, "'Tiger King' Co-Creator Says Racism from Joe Exotic Was Cut from Documentary," *NME*, April 7, 2020, www.nme.com/news/tv/tiger-king-joe-exotic-racism-cut-from-show-2642740
34. Horeck, *Justice on Demand*, 152.
35. As Prasad argues, there is "flippancy" in the way in "which the narrative lunges past the gravity of a young man's captivity to drug use, predatory love and attendant nihilism." See Prasad, "The Casual Boredom in *Tiger King*," 572.
36. Horeck, *Justice on Demand*, 138–9.
37. Stuart Joy, "Sexual Violence in Serial Form: *Breaking Bad* habits on TV," *Feminist Media Studies* 19, no. 1 (2019).
38. See Nygaard and Lagerwey, "*Tiger King's* Meme-ification."
39. Jason Mittell, *Complex TV: The Poetics of Contemporary Television Storytelling* (New York and London: New York University Press, 2015), 142.
40. Ibid.
41. Cited in James Poniewozik, *Audience of One: Donald Trump, Television, and the Fracturing of America* (New York: Liveright Publishing Corporation, 2019), 98.
42. Mittell, *Complex TV*, 348.
43. Poniewozik, *Audience of One*, 12.
44. Sundén and Paasonen, *Who's Laughing Now?*, 50.
45. Sarah Banet-Weiser, *Empowered: Popular Feminism and Popular Misogyny* (Durham and London: Duke University Press, 2018), 35.
46. In their mockery of white middle-aged femininity, Carole Baskin memes relate to the figure of the "Karen." Though the "Karen" meme initially emerged to call out racism and white privilege, critics suggest it has become detached from its critique of racist behaviors and is now often used to express a rote misogyny. See Diane Negra and Julia Leyda, "Querying 'Karen': The Rise of the Angry White Woman," *The European Journal of Cultural Studies*, published online 2020, doi:10.1177/1367549420947777
47. Amanda Taub, "A New Covid-19 Crisis: Domestic Abuse Rises Worldwide," *The New York Times*, April 6, 2020, www.nytimes.com/2020/04/06/world/coronavirus-domestic-violence.html
48. Cited in Ibid.
49. Debbie Ging and Eugenia Siapera, eds., "Special Issue on Online Misogyny," *Feminist Media Studies* 18, no. 4 (2018): 515–24.
50. Asaf Nissenbaum and Limor Shifman, "Meme Templates as Expressive Repertoires in a Globalizing World: A Cross-Linguistic Study," *Journal of Computer-Mediated Communication* 23 (2018): 295.

51. See Banet-Weiser, *Empowered*, 36 for a discussion of how misogyny gets read "as an anomaly" thus concealing how it "works as a norm."

52. As Caroline Bainbridge has argued, the psychodynamics of binge-viewing habits coax viewers to "stay with their selected show" but also with the "audiovisual paratexts aligned with it." See "Box-set Mind-set: Psycho-cultural Approaches to Binge Watching, Gender, and Digital Experience," *free associations*, no. 75 (June 2019): 65–83. ISSN: 2047–0622, www.freeassociations.org.uk/

53. Nissenbaum and Shifman, "Meme Templates," 306.

4 Labor, celebrity, and the carnivalesque world of *Tiger King*

Kate Fortmueller

On March 20, 2020, Netflix released *Tiger King: Murder, Mayhem and Madness* several days after the United States began to experience its own mayhem. As the coronavirus pandemic hit the United States and people across the country began to shelter in place, we became perhaps uniquely susceptible to viral television programming. *Tiger King*, with its collection of popular genre tags including docuseries, LGBTQ, and true crime, quickly jumped to the top of Netflix subscribers' home pages, wooing legions of people stuck in quarantine. The show became a huge hit for Netflix, reportedly garnering more US viewers than *Stranger Things 2*'s 10-day viewership record, and external analytics firms proclaimed *Tiger King* "Netflix's most popular US original of 2020."[1] Although the pandemic outlasted the series' popularity in the United States, in its earliest weeks, *Tiger King* dominated the cultural zeitgeist. Speaking to the *Los Angeles Times* about the success of *Tiger King*, director Rebecca Chaiklin commented: "I hope the series can provide a bit of entertainment and distraction for people, but more than anything, we're glad that people are staying home."[2]

Stuck in what we imagined (or at least hoped) would be a temporary lockdown, the norms of work, family life, and leisure were transformed. Many embraced the pandemic upheaval by adopting new hobbies, while others struggled to juggle work and caregiving labor. Regardless of how their lives were disordered by the pandemic, many turned to the chaotic world of *Tiger King* for entertainment. For audiences, part of the attraction of the show seemed to be its carnivalesque qualities. The term "carnivalesque," as derived from literary critic Mikhail Bakhtin, describes a literary mode that, like a carnival itself, upends cultural hierarchies and norms. It is a form of folk entertainment and humor that encourages visitors to embrace a new set of rules for a brief period of time. In the case of *Tiger King*, the carnivalesque manifests in individual eccentricities, rule breaking by the various big cat owners and exhibitors, employment and employee relations at all the zoos, as well as the show's form, which embraces some of the vernacular of

DOI: 10.4324/9781003157205-5

reality television and celebrity-driven media. Formally, the series exploits these carnivalesque aspects to present the topsy-turvy world of independent zoos around the United States.

However, the docuseries' representation of labor pushes back at the idea of *Tiger King* as a free, carnivalesque space. The performance labor of the main subjects and the capitalized labor of the underpaid employees and unpaid interns working in these zoos that seem shocking on the surface are very much a part of the neoliberal status quo. Like the pandemic, *Tiger King* laid bare many of the differences between individuals' professional lives. As people sheltered in place around the United States, they also experienced an unsettling shift in the norms of work, time, and social interaction. Many of those who could work from home took cues from internet celebrities to upgrade their home offices and craft professional mise-en-scènes with ring lights and higher-quality microphones. In contrast, essential workers, such as those in medical or sanitation fields, food processing, or grocery store employees, found themselves taking greater risks without increased compensation. Even as the public became more aware of these labor differences in society, *Tiger King* represented neoliberal labor in spectacular microcosm. Audiences were glued to their screens watching Joe Exotic, Carole Baskin, and Bhagavan "Doc" Antle build their big cat brands while relying on the capitalized labor of underpaid workers and unpaid interns to care for the animals and their surrounding environments.

Tiger King features many colorful characters, but Joe Schreibvogel-Maldonado-Passage (aka "The Tiger King" aka "Joe Exotic," as I will refer to him henceforth) is clearly the star of the series. Joe Exotic is an entrepreneur who purchased the G.W. Zoo (named for Joe Exotic's deceased brother, Garold Wayne) in 1997 and developed it into a multimedia ecosystem designed to promote his outsider persona. Joe Exotic is a P.T. Barnum-like late capitalist figure, a showman and entrepreneur with more tools at his disposal for self-promotion than Barnum could ever have imagined. He is a multiplatform celebrity: in addition to the zoo, Joe Exotic released music videos, ran the TV station Joe Exotic TV (Figure 4.1), and designed branded merchandise, including an underwear line; he also joined the crowded field of 2016 Republican Presidential candidates and later ran for Governor of Oklahoma. Prior to *Tiger King*, Joe Exotic had seemingly worked hard to achieve a level of regional infamy for his antics at the zoo, treatment of animals, and multiple husbands. The construction of an outrageous persona and a reliance on spectacle are key to both Barnum's and Joe Exotic's notoriety. As Bluford Adams said of Barnum, "His celebrity was his life's work and his prize possession. He bragged about it, sued people over it, threatened to kill it, but most

Figure 4.1 Inside Joe Exotic's reality television studio.

of all he reinvented it."³ These observations about Barnum anticipate the tumultuous stories of Joe Exotic's self-aggrandizing behavior, but they also manifest as somewhat typical behavior for contemporary microcelebrities. As Alice Marwick explains, microcelebrity is "something that one *does*, rather than something that one *is*."⁴ Marwick characterizes microcelebrity as a process by which practitioners carefully construct their own personae and "see their audience as fans rather than friends or family and share information strategically with this audience to boost their popularity and attention within a network."⁵ But, for Joe Exotic, as well as other featured subjects in the series like Doc Antle and Carole Baskin, their ability to actively cultivate their personae still relies on the physical space of the zoo to anchor their microcelebrity brand.

In the framing of their subjects, directors Eric Goode and Rebecca Chaiklin particularly embrace Joe Exotic's swagger and Doc Antle's pseudospiritualism, foregrounding the many ways that they use their charisma to cultivate carnivalesque environments at G.W. Zoo and Myrtle Beach Safari, respectively. Those who work and live in the social environments depicted in *Tiger King* profess that what drew them to their jobs was a desire to live a life unfettered by mainstream conventions. For those in charge of the zoos, hedonistic privileging of individual pleasure seems to take precedence over all else. However, while the culture of these zoos may upend certain norms, these transgressions are long term, unlike the temporary nature of a real carnival or the literary carnivalesque. Working with big cats and maintaining these zoos, as zoo owner Doc Antle explains, "is a lifestyle." Short-term transgressions flout rules, and in doing so, draw attention to the upended conventions. If rules or laws are openly disregarded for prolonged periods, old rules are simply replaced with new norms. When a carnivalesque culture crystallizes, it simply becomes another system with its own internal rules and controls.

Rather than looking at the docuseries as an oddity, then, it is more productive to consider the ways that it reflects mainstream cultural norms within neoliberal labor arrangements. Although *Tiger King* ostensibly presents us with central characters who make moral, legal, and (sometimes stunning) sartorial transgressions, their violations are merely superficial deviations from societal conventions that ultimately work in promotional service to their exotic microcelebrity personae. As a result, rather than offering an escape from Trump's America and the raging pandemic, *Tiger King* presents us, often uncritically, with a vision of labored entrepreneurial self-branding and a strutting performance of patriarchal American culture, neoliberal economic systems, and labor exploitation, all dressed up in animal print, distressed denim, and a bleach blonde mullet.

Tiger kingdoms, or the cult of the carnivalesque

Private zoos are ostensibly sites of entertainment akin to carnivals or amusement parks, but the exhibitors featured in the series run their zoos like miniature kingdoms, wielding power over the lives and livelihoods of their employees. Joe Exotic's G.W. Zoo is one of many private zoos in the United States operating on the margins as a permanent tourist attraction outside of a major city. As evidenced by a map in Episode 2, most of the locations of the big cat exhibitors around the United States are far from major cities in places like Myrtle Beach, SC, and Wynnewood, OK, keeping them safe from regulatory interference and mainstream cultural influence. In the Bakhtinian sense, carnivalesque behaviors are noteworthy because they are fixed to a limited period of time and a specifically delineated festive space. As Bakhtin explains, the carnival is "not a spectacle seen by the people; they live in it. . . . While carnival lasts, there is no other life outside it."[6] Carnivalesque is a term that seems uniquely well-suited to describe the various worlds of private zoos (not just G.W. Zoo) in *Tiger King* because many of the activities on screen subvert norms and exist outside of mainstream cultural mores. As the series shows, many of these big cat owners enjoy activities – beyond owning multiple exotic and endangered pets – that are made easier by their location in rural areas; for example, Joe Exotic enjoys taking target practice on mannequins, mattresses, and other domestic objects and blowing things up. While Bakhtin valorizes the liberatory possibilities for temporary transgressive spaces, when the carnivalesque crystallizes into a long-term installation, the liberatory potential may erode and the spaces bear a closer resemblance to cults and cult-like hierarchies.

As Rick Kirkham, producer of Joe Exotic TV, explains in the series: "People who worked for Joe were misfits [and he was] the King of the Misfits who reigned over them." Joe Exotic's employees who are interviewed in the series identify as outsiders who came to work in the zoo as a way to break the monotony of their lives and reject the constraints of mainstream society. The same can be said of some of the women who joined Doc Antle's zoo, such as Barbara Fisher, who left Iowa to work with animals, do yoga, and live a vegetarian lifestyle. Regardless of why people have been enticed to work in these zoos, the work is hazardous and exhausting. However, the employees and zoo owners position the opportunity to work with wild animals as a passion career which justifies these health risks. Several of the employees at G.W. Zoo sustained serious injuries and/or lost limbs from their work. Joe Exotic's workers are so poorly compensated that they pick through trucks of expired Walmart meat, the same undesirable food intended for the tigers. Workers at Doc Antle's zoo are paid $100 per week and sleep in stables, while Carole Baskin proudly announces that she doesn't pay people to work with animals because it is work people will do for free. Throughout the series, zoo owners, some of the workers, and many of the visitors interviewed all emphasize the appeal of petting and cuddling with tiger cubs. The intimate access to the animals flouts the rules of animal care and provides workers incentive to stay at the zoos. For those running these zoos, this affective component of the job supposedly helps compensate for the low pay and real dangers of the job, a rhetorical strategy that resembles work in media and production fields, wherein the creative outlet supposedly offsets the paltry compensation.[7] Although these zoos are on the margins of cities, their reliance on the "perks" of the job to justify low to no pay resonates with the logic of the glamorous entertainment industry and, more broadly, neoliberal capitalism. As Angela McRobbie explains, neoliberal institutions encourage workers to "bypass mainstream employment with its trade unions and trenches of welfare and protection in favour of the challenge and excitement of being a[n] . . . entrepreneur."[8] Work with large cats might appear exotic and outside the system, but the exploitative practices in this industry are commonplace strategies of 21st century capitalized labor.

To varying degrees, these big cat exhibitors have created their own cult-like spaces with distinct moral universes. Several of the zoos featured in *Tiger King* house their employees, which helps to isolate the workers from medical care, family, and friends. All the workers in these zoos and animal sanctuaries must embrace the environments established by owners like Joe Exotic, Bhagavan Doc Antle, and Carole Baskin. Sacrifices have varied at each zoo; Baskin asks people to work for low to no pay, and Doc Antle requires employees to get breast implants. Both Joe Exotic and Doc Antle maintain long-term polygamous relationships with people who came to work with them as teenagers. Although there are no interviews with Doc Antle's wives, and he dismisses questions about his personal life, there are clear indications that Joe Exotic's husbands may have been coerced into their thruple, most notably the fact that Travis Maldonado complained of feeling trapped on the compound and eventually committed suicide.

These zoos and the various big cat aficionados who run them adopt a kind of loose libertarian-ethos, violating numerous laws and shirking societal norms. There are laws prohibiting big cat sales and ownership around the United States, so simply participating in the world of big cats creates opportunities to engage with people who are on the legal fringes of society. One of the figures briefly featured in Episode 2 is Mario Tabraue, a former drug kingpin living on a gated property with monkeys and untold numbers of exotic animals. Director Eric Goode inserts himself into the series to explain the broader context of United States animal trafficking when he reveals that his exploration of venomous snake dealers introduced him to the world of big cat animal sales and led him to explore the worlds of Joe Exotic, Carole Baskin, Doc Antle, and others. Many interviewees imply that some of the central figures have participated in illegal cat trafficking, but this is not the only way that the interview subjects situate themselves outside of mainstream societal boundaries.

Employees do not seem to have much life outside of the tiger kingdoms. Most of the workers are paid extremely low wages and live on site, yet, the workers interviewed in *Tiger King*, apart from Barbara Fisher who left Doc Antle's employ, all project a tremendous amount of commitment to their employers. Several of the workers focus on the appeal of living outside of the system, but there seems to be little reflection on the terrible conditions, the dire health risks, and the ways that the seemingly onerous regulations of mainstream society are simply replaced with a new set of rules and behavioral norms within these zoos. Some such as Travis Maldonado and Fisher recognized these repressive cultures, but many others remained in thrall of their charismatic leaders, the carnivalesque culture, and the big cats that surrounded them.

Celebrity labor and the performance of authenticity

Unlike Bahktin's description of the antihierarchical carnivalesque environments, the zoos in *Tiger King* have clear leaders and many of the efforts of the workers are in service of the fame of the big personalities running the zoos. In the first episode, G.W. Zoo employee Kelci "Saff" Saffery quips:

"Joe was an entertainer by nature; he was pretty much the star of his own show." Even before *Tiger King*, we see ample evidence of Joe Exotic's desire for the spotlight. The "Joe Exotic" story first appeared in 2019 in *New York Magazine* and then was featured in Season 2 of the *Over My Dead Body* podcast series (titled "Joe Exotic: Tiger King"), which hit number one on the Apple podcast downloads.[9] While popular, the audio and textual forms of the Tiger King's pulpy story did not reach the viral success of the Netflix show. Prior to the release of *Tiger King*, Joe Exotic was not a household name, but he seemed undeterred in his quest for fame. As Saffery observes in Episode 1, "For Joe, the Zoo was his stage. . . . He controlled every aspect of it. From the start of the day to the end of the day, he filmed everything." Joe Exotic, like many niche celebrities, was able to capitalize on his notoriety through long-tail and multiplatform marketing strategies by producing inexpensive and surprisingly diversified content for a small audience. These efforts did not launch Joe Exotic into mass stardom, but he successfully used reality television, YouTube, and his zoo to attain modest fame outside of the mainstream media industries. Despite Joe Exotic's attempts to be a self-made celebrity, his status obviously changed dramatically in 2020 when Netflix gave him a global platform, which swiftly launched him into global reality star status.

Tiger King simultaneously showcases and effaces aspects of Joe Exotic's celebrity labor, a dualism that makes the docuseries complicit in Joe Exotic's starmaking, or, as he would likely say, kingmaking. As Thomas Waugh writes, "Documentary film in everyday commonsense parlance, implies the absence of the elements of performance, acting, staging, directing, etc."[10] Waugh is addressing documentary filmmaking practice generally, but these rules become complicated in the context of documentary projects that center on performers, celebrities, or other public figures who are hyperaware of their performance of themselves. Writing about rockumentaries, Priyadarshini Shanker stresses the importance of delineations between onstage performances and backstage shots, which focus on the "presentation of the star-as-worker."[11] In *Tiger King*, there are many displays of the labor of performance, such as the preening, costuming, and application of makeup. However, there are very few backstage moments in *Tiger King*, since much of the archival footage that Goode and Chaiklin draw from had been filmed for his reality series, in which Joe Exotic seemed to be performing a highly curated image of himself. According to Rick Kirkham, who produced the failed reality series, Joe Exotic embraced tropes of reality shows and tried to amplify the drama of his own. As Kirkham says in Episode 4, "He would have done anything to become famous. . . . I watched him fire people just because he knew the camera was rolling." Kirkham, who was also fired, is possibly a dubious source on this subject; however, this analysis of Joe

Exotic aligns with what we do observe in the few backstage moments of the film.

There are segments – mostly before interviews and surveillance shots – that provide some "backstage" access to both the image production of the characters and the documentary production more broadly. In *Tiger King*, the camera often lingers silently over posed interview subjects, positioning them in tableaus and placing these self-styled gurus on full display within a highly constructed mise-en-scène. In Episode 1, Eric Goode drives up to meet Carole Baskin and notes "she's dressed perfectly," indicating his approval as if he was validating the choices of a costume director. Carole Baskin walks toward the camera wearing a flower crown and a pink and orange patchworked animal print blouse asking questions about her positioning and framing before kneeling and launching into her explanation of the lion in the background (Figure 4.2). The combination of Goode's comment and Baskin's actions is just one example in this series of how directors and subjects collaborate on costume, framing, and staging thereby supporting the microcelebrity self-branding of Joe Exotic, Baskin, and Antle. The emphasis on appearance permeates Episode 1, for example, as the *Tiger King* production team prepares Joe Exotic for his interview, and he expresses concern about removing his hat because he fears his mullet would scare the viewers. Given Joe Exotic's investment in being an outsider, there are two ways to interpret this moment: he could be genuinely self-conscious, or he could be explicitly drawing attention to his hair. Regardless of the moment's authenticity, both interpretations reveal Joe Exotic, and perhaps the film's, investment in his appearance. Doc Antle, in contrast, seems more invested in directing his own scenes as, in one scene, he explains to Goode that they

Figure 4.2 Carole Baskin looking "perfect" for her first appearance in the series.

should film him opening the door and welcoming Goode and the camera crew into his home.

Although *Tiger King* revels in the self-awareness of its subjects and their image production, in other ways, the documentary effaces some of the essential "backstage" labor performed by its stars. Perhaps, the most significant example of this is how the docuseries presents misleading information around Joe Exotic's musical career. When Joe Exotic talks about his music career as a country artist, his poorly lip-synced music videos are presented as evidence of his work.[12] Joe Exotic continually refers to "his music," but nobody in the documentary ever acknowledges that country singers Vince Johnson and Danny Clinton provide the vocals for his albums and music videos.[13] In fact, *Tiger King* indulges the illusion that Joe Exotic is a country singer. Episode 4 cold opens with Joe Exotic's music video for a song called "Bring it On," intercutting the footage with images of him singing in a recording studio. There is a sound bridge between the music video and a brief scene of Joe Exotic exiting the G.W. Zoo gift shop to get in his truck. As he drives, he explains in voice over: "I use my music as an escape from reality." The opening sequence is oddly misleading. His exit from the building along with his moment of reflection on "his music" suggests that he had been laying down tracks before getting into his pickup. This directorial choice – hiding the fact that Joe Exotic does not sing – bolsters Joe Exotic's image as a multitalented star, rather than revealing the many layers of his screen performance(s). Joe Exotic is never confronted with the fact that he lip-syncs nor is he asked to justify his need to pretend to have a musical career. The inclusion of moments of celebrity self-branding and exclusion of contextualizing information about Joe Exotic's music career make the docuseries complicit in his mythmaking.

Documentaries about performers, whether microcelebrity or superstar, confront layers of performance in the process of filming and exploring their subjects. In her discussion of a documentary about global superstar Shah Rukh Khan (who is, incidentally, also known for lip-syncing, a practice acknowledged and accepted within Bollywood films), Priyadarshini Shanker asks, "What is at stake when the documentary mode attempts to arrest the moment of star-production and record a star's confrontation with his own stardom? . . . what happens to the very concept of documentary and its cognates, such as 'reality' and 'authenticity,' when they confront the multiple levels of performance necessary to market a promotional material?"[14] In the case of *Tiger King*, the more relevant question might be: What happens when documentarians and their subjects do not confront the promotional practices of celebrities or stars? There are brief moments in which we see Joe Exotic and Carole Baskin fussing over their self-presentation and the production of their own images, albeit with seemingly different motives; Joe Exotic seems focused on his celebrity and Carole Baskin appears focused on establishing credibility. However, none of the subjects appears to confront the process of image production with anything other than self-satisfaction. By reveling in, rather than interrogating promotional practices, *Tiger King* blends aspects of celebrity culture into this documentary, making what Christie Milliken and Steve Anderson call, "concessions to fiction-based tendencies and the pleasures of the popular."[15]

Many of the strengths of documentaries, such as providing authentic access to unfamiliar or exotic subject matters, dovetail with the qualities that celebrity scholars have highlighted as the unique qualities of internet celebrities, such as their authenticity and distance from the legacy film and television industries.[16] However, while documentaries might project authenticity through self-conscious choices that draw attention to their construction, celebrities need to make sure that their veneer of authenticity is never punctured. Key to internet celebrity is a version of authenticity in which the onscreen persona matches the offscreen persona and is seemingly unmarred by agents, managers, or publicists who handle stars or Hollywood celebrities. By extension, these internet celebrities frequently possess a fundamentally different appeal to their fans. In her characterization of internet celebrity types, Crystal Abidin identifies the "exotic" celebrity who "is perceived as distancing, far removed from one's comfort zone, or so novel or foreign that it piques the interest of audiences who hold contrasting or different forms of 'cultural capital.'"[17] Abidin's analysis conforms with the fascination viewers have for Joe Exotic, Carole Baskin, and Doc Antle, all of whom inhabit and rule over their own carefully constructed outsider communities. Despite formal affinities between documentary and internet celebrity, documentary filmmaking is associated with higher levels of transparency than is common in celebrity-produced content in service of an individual brand. *Tiger King* does not always paint flattering portraits of its subjects. But, Joe Exotic's celebrity brand is based on controversy and a disregard for social mores, so the series did not need to be flattering; it just needed to be consistent with his public-facing image. Thus, it seems fitting that Joe Exotic was delighted by the series and its success. In response to a phone conversation with Joe Exotic, Eric Goode explains in an interview, "[Joe Exotic] has lived his entire life just to be famous and so to finally realise this fame is just . . . He's tickled pink . . . He's absolutely thrilled."[18] Absent an investigatory approach into who Joe Exotic is (and perhaps what informs his decisions), a critical lens, or even a willingness to acknowledge some of Joe Exotic's lies, half-truths, and self-promotion as such, documentaries like *Tiger King* accede to Joe Exotic's image of himself and contribute to the faux carnivalesque world and the construction of his larger brand.

Conclusion

On March 20, 2021, Netflix commemorated the one-year anniversary of *Tiger King's* release on Twitter, commenting: "Looking back, it feels like Tiger King was the perfect series to match the mood of March 2020 – it was like nothing we'd ever seen before, nothing quite made sense, and we didn't know exactly how it would end."[19] I agree with the Netflix social media team in its assertion that the series seemed to match the national mood. For millions of people, *Tiger King* was part of a quarantine fad, whether they watched the show, experienced the narrative through memes, boosted its popularity through one of many social media conversations, or took a *Tiger King*-themed virtual workout. However, *Tiger King* also exemplified many long-standing and regrettable elements of celebrity culture and labor conditions in the United States beyond the pandemic context.

Tiger King showcases two forms of neoliberal labor: performance and capitalized labor. Although these two forms are often separated, and they are treated differently in the series, both forms are also imbricated. In the cases of Joe Exotic and Doc Antle, the labor of the zoo workers is essential to maintaining their carnivalesque worlds that are essential to their own celebrity brands. The culture they create at the zoos is an essential part of their public personae and provides a testament to their charisma. While these forms of labor are deeply connected, the series showcases minimal performance labor and more openly presents the exploitation of the zoo workers.

As a docuseries about animal abuse and crime, the narrative functions to show how Joe Exotic, Carole Baskin, and Doc Antle rely on their wild animals to cultivate celebrity and grow their personal brands. Instead of igniting an animal rights movement to save the big cats, solving the murder of Carole Baskin's husband, or helping to get Joe Exotic released from prison, the show reifies neoliberal economic conditions. Joe Exotic, Doc Antle, and, to some extent, Carole Baskin all have clearly crafted personas and images, which are often underscored by the show's presentational style. Moments when the camera lingers on Joe Exotic, Doc Antle, and Carole Baskin do not necessarily reveal aspects of their authentic selves, but rather the extent to which all these figures are contemplating and strategizing their individual images as "outsiders." Joe Exotic and Doc Antle in particular craft their celebrity personae around their roles as ringleaders of outsider zoo culture, and they use the wild animals in these zoos to cultivate intimacy with workers and exploit purported devotion to the animals to maintain relationships with the underpaid workers who bolster their images as big cat entrepreneurs. Chock full of self-made business owners, the characters in *Tiger King* position themselves as iconoclasts, but when it comes to their desire for money and power, they are decidedly American capitalists.

Notes

1. Gavin Bridge, "'Tiger King' Is Netflix's Most Popular U.S. Original of 2020," *Variety+*, December 28, 2020, https://variety.com/vip/tiger-king-is-netflixs-most-popular-u-s-original-of-2020–1234874574/
2. Amy Kaufman, "Imprisoned 'Tiger King' Star Joe Exotic Is 'Over the Moon' to Be Famous, Directors Say," *Los Angeles Times*, March 26, 2020, www.latimes.com/entertainment-arts/tv/story/2020-03-26/joe-exotic-tiger-king-netflix-burning-questions
3. Bluford Adams, *E Pluribus Barnum: The Great Showman & The Making of U.S. Popular Culture* (Minneapolis, MN: University of Minnesota Press, 1997), 1.
4. Alice Marwick, "You May Know Me From YouTube: (Micro-) Celebrity in Social Media," in *A Companion to Celebrity*, eds. P. David Marshall and Sean Redmond (Malden, MA: Wiley and Sons, 2015), 337.
5. Ibid.
6. Mikhail Bakhtin, *Rabelais and His World*, translated by Hélène Iswolsky (Bloomington, IN: Indiana University Press, 1986), 7.
7. For more on affective labor and laborers, see: Brooke Erin Duffy, *(Not) Getting Paid to Do What You Love* (New Haven, CT: Yale University Press, 2017).
8. Angela McRobbie, *Be Creative* (Cambridge: Polity, 2016), 11.
9. Robert Moor, "American Animals," *New York Magazine*, September 3, 2019, https://nymag.com/intelligencer/2019/09/joe-exotic-and-his-american-animals.html; Robert Moor, *Joe Exotic: Tiger King, Wondery*, https://wondery.com/shows/joe-exotic/; Joshua Dudley, "Season 2 of 'Over My Dead Body' Brings True Crime Drama to a 'Wild' New Dimension," *Forbes*, August 31, 2019, www.forbes.com/sites/joshuadudley/2019/08/31/season-2-of-over-my-dead-body-brings-true-crime-drama-to-a-wild-new-dimension/?sh=3d470fca4291
10. Thomas Waugh, "Acting to Play Oneself: Notes on Performance in Documentary," in *Making Visible the Invisible: An Anthology of Original Essays on Film Acting*, ed. Carole Zucker (Metuchen, NJ: The Scarecrow Press, 1990), 66.
11. Priyadarshani Shanker, "Star Gazing via Documentary," *Framework: The Journal of Cinema and Media* 58, nos. 1–2 (Spring/Fall 2017): 112.
12. August Brown, "Did 'Tiger King' Star Joe Exotic Really Sing Those Jaw-Dropping Country Songs?" *Los Angeles Times*, March 24, 2020, www.latimes.com/entertainment-arts/music/story/2020-03-24/tiger-king-joe-exotic-netflix-country-songs-here-kitty-kitty
13. Julie Miller, "*Tiger King:* Inside Joe Exotic's Wild Homemade Music Videos," *Vanity Fair*, March 23, 2020, www.vanityfair.com/hollywood/2020/03/netflix-tiger-king-joe-exotic
14. Shanker, "Star Gazing via Documentary," 106.
15. Christie Millikan and Steve Anderson, "The Work of Popular Documentary in the Age of Alternative Facts," *Reclaiming Popular Documentary* (Bloomington, IN: Indiana University Press, 2021), 4.

16. For an excellent discussion of the qualities of internet and microcelebrities, see Alice Marwick, *Status Update: Celebrity, Publicity, and Branding in the Social Media Age* (New Haven, CT: Yale University Press, 2013), 115–23.

17. Crystal Abidin, *Internet Celebrity: Understanding Fame Online* (Bingley: Emerald Publishing House, 2018), 22.

18. Jess Hardiman, "Documentary Responds to Carole Baskin's Backlash," *LAD-Bible*, March 27, 2020, www.ladbible.com/entertainment/tv-and-film-director-behind-tiger-king-documentary-responds-to-carole-baskin-20200327

19. *Netflix*, March 20, 2021, 12:54 pm, https://twitter.com/netflix/status/137331 6948872687618

5 "I'm in a cage"

A historical perspective on *Tiger King*'s animals

Vanessa Bateman

Directors Rebecca Chaiklin and Eric Goode were profiling a snake dealer in South Florida for a documentary project when they came across a man who had just purchased a snow leopard. In the first episode of *Tiger King*, we see the leopard crouching in a dog crate in the back of a cargo van with the words "Wildlife Sanctuary" painted on its side. In the 100-degree heat, Goode casually asks the owner if the snow leopard is more common than a clouded leopard; "these are rarer," he says proudly. That chance encounter with a snow leopard, Goode explains, sent them down a five-year exploration of the world of big cat ownership in the United States and resulted in the seven-part documentary series *Tiger King: Murder, Mayhem and Madness* (2020). As the founder and president of the Turtle Conservancy, a nonprofit global conservation organization dedicated to protecting threatened and endangered turtles and tortoises, it was natural for Eric Goode to leverage his environmentalist experience for a project that would "expose the exploitation and the suffering" that animals in captivity face in the United States.[1] However, following *Tiger King*'s release, wildlife journalist Rachel Nuwer noted that many of the film's interview subjects were disappointed that the series did not follow in the tradition of a conservation documentary by doing more to expose the problem of the big cat industry. As she explains, they were told it would be "the big cat version of *Blackfish*," the scathing documentary concerning SeaWorld's orca, Tilikum, which claimed that killer whales become unnaturally aggressive due to the psychological damage inflicted by forced captivity.[2] CNN's broadcast of *Blackfish* (Gabriela Cowperthwaite, 2013) raised a public concern about the captivity of marine mammals and had real consequences for SeaWorld Entertainment Inc., including boycotts, loss of ticket sales, and decline in stock prices; the company even announced it would end killer whale shows and breeding programs (although it should be noted that, as of 2021, SeaWorld still runs orca performances).[3] Instead of pursuing a similar activist approach, *Tiger King* focused on the uncouth human dramas unfolding around the world

DOI: 10.4324/9781003157205-6

of big cat ownership, with an overarching story line about the downfall of roadside zookeeper Joseph Maldonado-Passage and his rivalry with Carole Baskin, founder of the sanctuary Big Cat Rescue. As Joshua Dial, who worked for Maldonado-Passage, aptly summarizes in the series' seventh episode:

> What started out as this feud between two people, a good and noble fight to stop cub selling, cub petting, turned into a personal and legal court battle, and it just became about them. . . . We've completely lost sight and lost touch of what really matters here, and that's the conservation and protection of the species of this planet.

Thus, the character-driven, true-crime narrative in *Tiger King* ultimately overshadows any focus on current issues of conservation and captivity, demonstrating an interest in, and preference for, the human subject over the animal.

Toward the end of the series, Maldonado-Passage, former zookeeper of the Greater Wynnewood Exotic Animal Park (G.W. Zoo) and once the most prolific breeder of tigers in the United States, finds himself in the position he once reserved for his cats. "I'm in a cage," we hear him say via phone from the federal prison where he is currently serving 22 years for 17 charges of animal abuse and two counts of attempted murder for hire. On screen, the face of a tiger behind a wire cage is used as the background to this audio – drawing a visual parallel between zoos and prisons (Figure 5.1). Maldonado-Passage continues, "Do you know why animals die in cages? Their soul dies." G.W. Zoo is now closed to the public, but during its operation, the zoo had between 180 and 200 big cats, oftentimes keeping ten or more tigers in a cage at once, a far cry from their solitary long range in the wild. The captive tigers featured in the docuseries are part of a nationwide estimated population of 5,000–10,000, more than double the remaining 2,000–3,000 that roam free in the wild.[4] While *Tiger King* presents these staggering numbers as a direct result of breeders like Maldonado-Passage, the current population of exotic animals in American zoos, research labs, game ranches, and private homes are in fact the result of an almost two-century-long history of collecting and breeding animals in the United States.

There is a paradox, however, in historicizing animals. As animal studies scholar Erica Fudge explains, "If our only access to animals in the past is through documents written by humans, then we are never looking at animals, only ever at the representation of the animals by humans."[5] In the context of species in captivity that are threatened, endangered, or extinct in the wild, these animals are only encountered by humans through

Figure 5.1 A tiger gazes at the camera while its former zookeeper, Joe Maldonado-Passage, laments from prison, "I'm in a cage" (*Tiger King*, 2020).

modes of display or documentation. These various forms of exotic animal display and exhibition reveal a long history of morally and ethically fraught human–animal relations. It is a history of contradiction: animals are regarded as "wild," yet their breeding in captivity to supply consumers, Susan Nance proposes, has moved them into the realm of agriculture.[6] This contradiction emerged from a shift that occurred in the 20th century in society's attitudes toward wild animals, from a traditional "respectful coexistence at a distance, spiked here and there with hateful campaigns of extermination, to fascinated commodification."[7] Animals were also decontextualized from their exotic wild origins and recast as pets and entertainment in popular culture and by tourist venues like Las Vegas. *Tiger King* documents how animals today continue to be subjected to the consequences of our ever-changing conceptualization of them. The series exposes how extreme the commoditization of big cats has become in recent decades and the struggle between conceptualizing animals as property and attempting to reclaim an understanding of them as wild animals. By examining historical and species-specific perspectives on exotic animals in captivity, this chapter provides a broader context to the overlooked animals of *Tiger King* to demonstrate how past tendencies of collecting, exhibiting, and breeding can inform our reading of the docuseries and the world of big cat ownership in the United States.

Collecting and exhibiting animals

Exotic animals made their debut in the American colonies when a lion was brought to Boston, Massachusetts, in 1716, followed by a camel in 1721, and a polar bear in 1733; it was not until 1806 that the first tiger arrived in New York.[8] In the mid-18th century, it became common for sea captains to transport exotic animals to America with the hopes of making a profit and thus began the steady importation of exotic animals until the mid-20th century. To ensure the investment was profitable, cargo needed to be kept alive during the long voyage overseas during which animals experienced dire conditions. Unfortunately, the quality of life of these "abducted creatures" did not improve upon their arrival, and many animals did not live long in captivity.[9] The deceased inventory was accepted by the first public natural history museums that were opening at the end of the 19th century, exhibiting these animals as taxidermy.[10] As the quality of animal care significantly improved by the mid-20th century, zoo specimens of the past that had been fed poor diets and lived sedentary lives were considered "unsatisfactory representatives" of their species by the same natural history museums.[11]

Before the establishment of modern public zoos, the traveling menagerie was a way for the public to see wild animals firsthand; these became a major feature of circuses in the United States from the 1870s through the 1940s. On their way to and from the main performance in the "big top," audiences would pass through a collection of decorative wagons and portable corrals that were usually arranged in a rectangle. Displayed in the center would be the larger uncaged animals such as camels, zebras, and elephants; some large circuses held rarer animals such as rhinoceroses or giraffes. Together with the nation's first public parks and gardens, the first zoos were established in the late 19th and early 20th centuries as part of the urban landscape. The mode of displaying zoo animals was similar to that of the traveling menagerie: optimal viewing of animals meant their enclosures were designed with the spectator, not the animal, in mind. It was not until well into the second half of the 20th century that zoos changed their justification for keeping animals to a conservationist and educational rationale and made a significant effort to create the illusion that animals were living in their natural habitats through the architecture, landscape design, and soundscapes that we find in most public zoos today.

At the end of the 19th century and into the early 20th century, the number of circuses and zoos surged in the United States, a proliferation that coincided with the success of animal dealers who supplied the demand for exotic animals. To fill zoo and menagerie cages across the country, instead of sending out expeditions for specimens like most natural history museums were doing at the time, it was more affordable to ask local collectors, dealers, and owners of game preserves to supply them with animals. To get a sense of how many animals were being shipped into the country, consider that between 1880 and 1930, more than 650 animal shows took place, including circuses, Wild West, and dog and pony shows, and that during the same period, zoos increased from four to over 100.[12] Elizabeth Hanson explains that, as the popularity of exotic animals grew in the 19th century, animal collectors and dealers of live wild animals "rose in social status from obscure, marginal figures to heroes of popular culture."[13] Joe Maldonado-Passage's rise to fame reflects this trajectory; although he was well known as a prolific dealer of tigers in the world of big cat ownership before his arrest, to the public, he followed a path from regional personality to international fame as a result of the release of *Tiger King*. Like Maldonado-Passage, animal dealers and collectors throughout history have gained national recognition by chronicling their expedition adventures in books and films, usually with an underlying message aligned with modern colonialism that asserted white man's rightful dominance over the natural world. There was prestige associated with live animal collectors and hunters who continued the tradition of supplying American institutions with animals for the purpose of building scientific collections and creating animal displays as entertainment. President Theodore Roosevelt and his expedition hunting party, for example, brought back over 11,000 animal specimens (including 1,000 skins of large mammals) from the Smithsonian-Roosevelt African Expedition in Central and East Africa in 1910.[14] According to his own estimates, in three decades, American Frank Buck delivered 10,000 live mammals and 100,000 live birds to the United States and beyond to supply zoos and circuses; his collecting expeditions were chronicled in bestselling books such as *Bring 'Em Back Alive* (1930) and several wildlife documentaries in which he staged fights between different types of animals.[15] This interest in collecting exotic animals has persisted, with the United States Department of Agriculture licensing over 2,800 "animal exhibitors" in 2021, with only 241 of them accredited by the American Association of Zoos & Aquariums (AZA), an organization that requires high standards of animal care as well as scientific and conservation research and education.[16]

When the US Congress passed three endangered species acts between 1966 and 1973, including the Animal Welfare Act, which mandated standards of care for zoo animals, it reflected a changing public opinion about animal trade and exhibition. While large urban zoos increasingly updated their modes of exhibiting, collecting, and caring for their animals during this time, there were smaller zoos that continued to follow in the tradition of the traveling menagerie. These two distinct modes of displaying animals have continued today. For instance, there are large, accredited institutions, such as the San Diego Zoo, which are internationally respected for their exhibits, as well as their contributions to research, education, and conservation. There are also unaccredited zoos, often called roadside zoos, like the G.W. Zoo, which place emphasis on entertainment and spectacle and offer pay-to-play experiences for visitors to touch animals. "Roadside zoo" is a term generally used to indicate the poor quality of a facility because it is associated with accusations of cruelty or neglect; these spaces are generally found in rural locations and are usually less regulated. The roadside zoos featured in *Tiger King* claim legitimacy by posing as members of fake organizations or incorrectly referring to their for-profit zoos as wildlife preserves or sanctuaries. For example, the G.W. Zoo declared it was accredited by the United States Zoological Association, a corporation formed by Maldonado-Passage in 2008, and Tim Stark's zoo, deceptively called Wildlife in Need, falsely claimed to be a nonprofit.[17] Doc Antle founded The Institute for Greatly Endangered and Rare Species (T.I.G.E.R.S.), an acronym for his Myrtle Beach Safari, which claims it is a "wildlife tropical preserve." A nature preserve is generally a protected area of undeveloped land that is reserved and managed for the purposes of conservation of flora and fauna that are native to that region. Antle's breeding of tigers through "a program run by the Species Survival Trust" is a misleading name for their in-house breeding practice, and it is not the legitimate Species Survival Program run by the AZA.

Whether public or private, however, zoos are always ethically fraught spaces. In examining the evolution of the relationship between humans and animals, John Berger reveals how an ancient and "unspeakable companionship" has been lost in our late-capitalist society. The zoo, he argues, is the place where animals are the most marginalized; it is the monument to our complicated relationship with them. As he explains, "Public zoos came into existence at the beginning of the period which was to see the disappearance of animals from daily life. The zoo to which people go to meet animals, to observe them, to see them, is, in fact, a monument to the impossibility of such encounters."[18] Our expectation of an authentic encounter with animals in captivity is often about how the animal reacts to our own presence. The "fantasy of human contact with non-human animals" is documented throughout *Tiger King* as people interact with animals in intimate ways, including visitors who pay high prices to handle tiger cubs and get their photographs taken with them.[19] These scenes record what Nigel Rothfels observes about zoos: "[w]e seem intent to catch the look of an animal, to see the animal look at us."[20] But as Berger writes, the reason zoo animals are "less than [we] believed" is because they resist looking at us.[21] Randy Malamud observes that zoo animals are "sad animals, constrained animals, displaced animals," yet zoo visitors are persuaded "to pretend they are looking at real animals."[22] There is a parallel, Berger argues, between viewing animals in a zoo and art in a gallery; zoo visitors move from cage to cage, stopping momentarily to look at animals on display who have been framed by their enclosure, "Yet in the zoo the view is always wrong. Like an image out of focus."[23] Similarly, Malamud equates the zoo experience to window shopping at a mall, moving through a space that is designed for the "ease and convenience of people."[24]

Through the gridded filter of metal wire, tigers and leopards growl and snarl, seemingly provoked by the camera, as *Tiger King*'s dialogue track remains focused on the human drama around these animals. These images are used on a perpetual playback loop; a visual metaphor to reinforce the "animality" of the human characters, the tigers are rarely represented as subjects themselves who might return the gaze of the viewer. The framing and fragmentation of animals in *Tiger King*, however, disrupts a transparent viewing of zoo animals, in part because facilities like the G.W. Zoo represent an outdated model for displaying zoo animals. While large, urban zoos make use of elaborate landscaping and architecture to create the illusion that animals live in their natural habitat, roadside zoo animals are viewed *through* the screen of their caged or barred enclosures. Chaiklin and Goode accentuate the confines of captivity by filming from outside these enclosures. The inclusion of metal cage or fencing that keep animal and human separate reminds viewers of the animals' displacement from any resemblance of a natural habitat. Many scenes feature close shots that fill the screen; sometimes, we are not sure if these are animals in Joe Madonado-Passage's G.W. Zoo or Carole Baskin's Big Cat Rescue – does it matter? Either way, these scenes visually represent how Berger interprets the experience of the zoo visitor: "you are looking at something that has been rendered absolutely marginal."[25]

Another way in which *Tiger King* diverges from the curated experience of visiting a large, urban zoo is by providing viewers a glimpse of the captive animal experience, exposing how viewing exotic animals up close is not worth the price of their captivity. Most of the film's subjects declare their love for animals; meanwhile, we see instances of animals resisting interactions with these same people by instinctually biting or clawing them. In one scene, a staff member of the G.W. Zoo loses part of their arm from a tiger bite yet continues to work there because of a felt affinity with the animals. Viewers bear witness to multiple occurrences of animal abuse and neglect in the series, including alligators burned to death and big cats teased, prodded, fed rotten meat, pulled through a chain link fence minutes after birth, and smuggled in suitcases. There are several instances of guns being fired near animals or used to control their behavior. As part of an investigation into wildlife offenses, viewers observe the uncovering of tiger remains that were buried on zoo property after being illegally shot by Maldonado-Passage. Multiple allegations are made that tiger cubs are put down or disappear once they grow too large to be safely handled by the public. In *Tiger King*, then, the supposed progress that has been made in the treatment of captive animals since the early days of their import and display is revealed as a fiction.

Breeding the exotic

Throughout *Tiger King*, some interview subjects justify breeding and exhibiting animals as a way to save them from extinction. For example, private zoo owner Tim Stark, who, since the release of *Tiger King*, has been permanently forbidden from owning or exhibiting any exotic or native animals after violating the Animal Welfare Act more than 100 times, states: "What's the first thing you should do to protect an endangered species? Make more, not eliminate the source."[26] In reality, US born tigers like those in the G.W. Zoo are considered genetically "generic" because they are captive-bred intersubspecific crossed animals, meaning they are not identifiable as members of specific subspecies (such as Bengal or Siberian). Therefore, they have no conservation value.

Unlike more traditional wildlife conservation documentaries or nature films, *Tiger King* fails to provide information from a nonbiased authoritative perspective. There is no fact checking of commentary from interview subjects that is incorrect or misleading. Sanctuary operator Carole Baskin initially seems to fulfill the role of outside expert on the topic of captive breeding, but her apparent expertise is undermined in the third episode, which is dedicated to her alleged involvement in the disappearance of her husband. By framing Baskin as a villain, just as Maldonado-Passage does, the docuseries creates skepticism of her opinion and the efforts she has made to lobby for the Big Cat Public Safety Act, which would prohibit individuals from buying and owning large cats and ban direct public contact with them. In this regard, *Tiger King* once again privileges the human drama at the center of this story and therefore misses the opportunity to explain why excessive breeding of tigers to supply animals for the cub petting industry is unnatural, unethical, and detrimental to wildlife conservation.

While the USDA allows cubs to be handled by the public between eight and 12 weeks of age, animal protection attorney Carney Anne Nasser argues the cub petting industry has "enabled unscrupulous breeding practices with no oversight, contributed to a surplus number of captive tigers that is unascertainable with any degree of accuracy, and increased the likelihood that an increasing number of tiger parts entering the illegal trade will originate in the U.S."[27] Most roadside zoos and private owners keep no records of their animals, not just during their lifetime, but even after their death. Dead tigers are still valuable, perhaps more valuable, if their parts are funneled into the black market, which in turn perpetuates a cycle by creating a demand for tiger parts and encourages poaching. In other words, breeding tigers in captivity directly impedes their population in the wild.

The excessive breeding of white tigers in the past 50 years exemplifies how far big cats have moved from a traditional understanding of them as rare exotic creatures to becoming objects of cultural and economic value. White tigers are prominently featured throughout all seven episodes of *Tiger King*, illustrating how these exotic animals went from rare to commonplace, from national treasures to roadside attractions – from wild animals to objects of American popular culture. The detrimental and dangerous breeding practices used to create these animals for the purpose of human use is a testament to the marginalization of animals that Berger discusses. White tigers are produced through generations of inbreeding, which has reduced their genetic variability; their color is a result of a recessive mutation of a single gene, and if two copies of this gene are bred together, the resulting cub might express the trait. Breeding white tigers is considered unethical since many animals suffer health issues including body or facial abnormalities such as club feet, elongated heads, or crossed eyes, as seen in several of the white tigers featured in *Tiger King*.[28] Historically, white tigers are extremely rare in the wild since the genes responsible are represented by 0.001% of the population; however, the disproportionate ratio of white tigers to regular tigers in captivity is a result of relentless, intentional inbreeding.[29]

All white tigers in the United States, including the ones appearing in *Tiger King*, are related to a Bengal tiger named Mohan that was captured as a cub in India by the Maharaja of Rewa in 1951.[30] To produce more white tigers, Mohan was experimentally bred with one of his offspring, resulting in a litter of four white cubs since his daughter also carried the white gene. One of these cubs became the first white tiger in the United States after John Kluge, a German-American billionaire, donated money for the Smithsonian National Zoological Park to purchase one of these rare animals. For $10,000, Mohini the "Enchantress of Rewa" was selected by zoo director Theodore Reed who had traveled to India in 1961, accompanied by a *National Geographic* photographer.[31] After Mohini's purchase, India banned the exportation of any white tigers. Two-year-old Mohini was "the only white tiger in any zoo in the world" at the time and became an instant animal celebrity upon her arrival in the United States, presented to President Eisenhower on the lawn of the White House as "a gift to the children of America."[32]

The National Zoo's goal was for Mohini to produce the first generation of US born white tigers in an "attempt to preserve the white genetic factor."[33] The Smithsonian Institution celebrated Mohini's first litter containing a white cub – the first strain of white tigers in the country – by including a photo (Figure 5.2) and family tree in the 1964 *Annual Report of the Board of Regents of the Smithsonian Institution* to explain the inbreeding process. Inbreeding required to produce white tigers that carry the recessive gene mutation results in a complicated genealogy; when bred with Samson, both the half-brother and uncle of Mohini, they

Figure 5.2 Mohini of Rewa and two-month-old son, the first white tiger bred and born outside of India, National Zoological Park. *Annual Report of the Board of Regents of the Smithsonian Institution*, 1964.

Source: Courtesy of the Smithsonian Libraries and Archives.

produced a litter, resulting in Samson becoming the father, uncle, and great-uncle of his cubs and Mohini their mother, aunt, and great-aunt.[34] While these cubs were celebrated by the zoo, inbreeding was highly criticized in the press for the "danger of unfavorable side-effects" and early deaths.[35] Despite the risks, the zoo spent over a decade trying to produce more white tigers.[36] Both then and now, white tiger breeding is done for financial purposes; the difference today is that the practice is now condemned by AZA-accredited zoos, including the National Zoo, and these animals are no longer rare. In less than a century, white tigers have gone from being nationally celebrated for their rare exoticism to being regularly produced at roadside zoos.

The popularity of tiger cubs today in the United States can also be traced back to Mohini, who was highly publicized throughout the 1960s and 1970s, including a nationally broadcast film special in 1964 chronicling her voyage from the palace in India to the birth of her first litter. In official reports and press, emphasis was placed on assuring the public that she was "an exceptional mother" and how proper care was provided to her.[37] There was a hands-off approach with the birth of Mohini's cubs: the tiger was placed into a closed nesting box with a few peep holes and a closed-circuit television camera for zookeepers to keep watch. This sharply contrasts with a scene in *Tiger King* in which, moments after birth, a tiger cub is pulled from its mother through a chain-link fence, followed by a scene in the Maldonado-Passage home where we see the baby tiger and its litter mates in a playpen while he complains "they just never stop screaming."

White tigers today have different cultural associations and value than in the era of Mohini. They were rebranded from national treasure to American icons by the German-American illusionists and entertainers Siegfried Fischbacher (1939–2021) and Roy Horn (1944–2020), who performed with white lions and tigers for their Las Vegas show *Siegfried & Roy at the Mirage Resort and Casino* (1990–2003) until a tiger attacked Horn in front of a live audience.[38] No longer representatives of a successful national project, the white tigers featured throughout *Tiger King* manifest how their owners or breeders want to be seen by the public. Their striking appearance – the contrast of white and black stripes with blue eyes – is associated with exclusivity, yet at the same time, ownership and display of these animals is an imitation of the allure once associated with them. One cannot help but see visual similarities between Jeff Lowe and the cross-eyed white tiger that sits in the front seat of his convertible, a scene that has been used as promotional material for the series. For Lowe, white tigers and other big cats are symbolic of his perceived masculinity and prowess; he boasts in one scene of using these animals to lure women in

Las Vegas. In the hands of animal breeders like Lowe, the white tiger's original status has been denigrated.

Breeding white tigers or designer hybrids like tigons (offspring of male tiger and female lion) or ligers (offspring of male lion and female tiger) is exemplary of how zoos and exhibitors have pursued the exotic as a strategy for attracting visitors and national prestige. Within 50 years, white tiger breeding went from rare to commonplace and from a nationally celebrated to an unethical practice. The representation of these animals' specialness has changed as a result, and if the proposed Big Cat Public Safety Act is passed by Congress, we can assume that white tigers will become creatures of the past, regaining their elusiveness. While roadside zoos and private owners still breed novelty animals, these breeding practices are now banned by the AZA, who propose tigers only be bred through the Species Survival Plan in order to maintain genetically diverse and healthy populations of endangered animals for their zoos and for research and conservation purposes.[39] All this context is left out of *Tiger King*.

Yearning for companionship

Yet, part of the appeal of *Tiger* King is that many people do, regardless of their ethical commitments, long for wild animals. At the turn of the 20th century, the pervasiveness of exotic animals in US zoos, circuses, and films led to their increasing presence in the American family home as pets. It was relatively easy to purchase rare and imported species before the Endangered Species Act of 1973, if you were willing to pay high prices. A newspaper advertisement published in California in 1888 listed the cost of various animals: "a good male lion is worth $1000," the equivalent of over $27,000 today, and "a tiger $1200; leopards cost $350, for monkeys we pay $10 upwards according to species."[40] These purchases did not always turn out well. Frequently, these animals had to be donated to zoos or menageries. As an article in *McClure's Magazine* from 1900 warned, "The lion or tiger kitten that has been the pet of some private family . . . commonly returns to menagerie life accompanied by a message to this effect: 'Please take Kitty back; she has eaten the Mastiff'."[41] Likewise, today, many animals that end up in sanctuaries are from people who purchased them without fully understanding the risks, needs, or costs of care required for certain species. The Humane Society has compiled a document titled "Dangerous incidents involving bears, big cats and primates in the United States 1990–present" that is, as of early 2021, almost 200 pages long. The document collects headlines and USDA reports, such as "Capuchin monkey bites child petting her" (2018), "10-year-old N.C. boy killed by Bengal tiger" (2003), "Man mauled by pet bear" (2001), as well as several incidents at the G. W. Zoo.[42] Incidents like these have always occurred between humans and their pets; the only difference now is that exotic animals in the United States are often bought, sold, and owned illegally. Clearly, the Endangered Species Act has not stopped either the exotic animal trade or its negative consequences.

In the last decade, there have been several documentaries that have focused on exotic animal ownership, most of which demonstrate how people develop psychological dependence on their animals despite these wild creatures putting their owners, other people, or themselves in danger. Animal Planet's TV series *Fatal Attractions* (2010–2013) uses interviews and reenactments to recount cautionary stories about people sharing their homes with exotic animals, such as big cats, bears, and reptiles. As a sort of precursor to *Tiger King*, the documentary *The Elephant in the Living Room* (Michael Webber, 2010) addressed the controversy surrounding exotic pet ownership in the United States from the perspectives of an Ohio police officer and a man who struggled with owning two lions. *Ming of Harlem: Twenty One Storeys in the Air* (Phillip Warnell, 2014) documents the story of a 500-pound tiger, Ming, that lived in a five-bedroom apartment in a large public housing complex in Harlem. Ming's existence became known to authorities after his owner, Antoine Yates, went to the emergency room with bites on his arms and legs. When police confiscated the tiger, they also discovered a five-and-a-half-foot alligator; both had been living in the same apartment where Yates' mother would babysit children. *The Tiger Next Door* (Camilla Calamandrei, 2009) focuses on Dennis Hill, a backyard tiger breeder in Indiana (who makes a brief appearance in *Tiger King*) as he loses his license to keep animals, drawing larger connections with the epidemic of wild animal keeping and the black market for their parts.

All these documentaries highlight how common exotic animals are in the United States and how the ways animals are understood, displayed, bought, and sold reveal more about us than them. Moreover, their stories demonstrate how human–animal relationships are fraught with contradictions. *Tiger King* highlights the yearning some individuals have for meaningful relationships with exotic animals, even though, as Berger reminds us, this desire cannot be mutual. The steady transformation of exotic animals from "powerful, fast, and proud" in the wild to "slow, powerless, [and] domesticated" in captivity is captured in *Tiger King*, where we witness how, as Malamud explains, "In taking away the animals' power and freedom and beauty, we have somehow taken it on for ourselves."[43] Variously, animals are conceptualized in the series as property, objects of economic promise, symbols of prestige, or creatures that need refuge from human exploitation.

Throughout each episode of *Tiger King*, animal neglect is documented and exposed to the viewer-bystander, who has little agency to do anything about these abuses. Instead, the incarceration of Maldonado-Passage in the series' final episode brings a sense of retribution to what is witnessed on screen, a zookeeper behind bars just like his animals.

Notes

1. Adam Horton, "Murder, Madness and Tigers: Behind the Year's Wildest Netflix Series," *The Guardian*, March 20, 2020.
2. Rachel Nuwer, "'Tiger King' May Be Dangerous for Big Cats," *New York Times*, April 14, 2020.
3. SeaWorld Credit Rating, "Stocks Plummet in Response to 'Blackfish," *Chicago Tribune*, August 14, 2014; Kevin Roose, "SeaWorld: Remember When We Said That Blackfish Movie Didn't Hurt Us? Well, Never Mind," *New York Magazine*, August 13, 2014.
4. While the final title card of *Tiger King* estimates "5,000–10,000 tigers live in captivity in the US. Fewer than 4,000 tigers remain in the wild," the IUCN Red List of Threatened Species estimates there are only 2,100–3,100 mature individuals in the wild. J. Goodrich et al., "*Panthera Tigris*: Tiger," *IUCN Red List of Threatened Species*, 2015, https://dx.doi.org/10.2305/IUCN.UK.2015-2.RLTS.T15955A50659951.en
5. Erica Fudge, "A Left-Handed Blow: Writing the History of Animals," in *Representing Animals*, ed. Nigel Rothfels (Indianapolis, IN: Indiana University Press, 2002), 6.
6. Susan Nance et al., "Roundtable: Animal History in a Time of Crisis," *Agricultural History* 94, no. 3 (Summer 2020): 444–84, 459.
7. Ibid., 459.
8. Vernon N. Kisling, "Zoological Gardens of the United States," in *Zoo and Aquarium History: Ancient Animal Collections to Zoological Gardens* (New York: CRC Press, 2001), 147–8.
9. Nance et al., "Roundtable," 459.
10. The New York Zoological Park, or Bronx Zoo, for example donated "rare and valuable" animals for taxidermic and research purposes to the American Museum of Natural History. *Annual Report of the New York Zoological Society*, Vol. 7 (New York: New York Zoological Society, 1902).
11. The afterlife of zoo animals in museum collections maintains the idea that there is scientific and educational value of keeping animals in captivity. James D. Olson and Donald R. Patten, "Museum-Zoo Relations and the Arabian Oryx," *Terra: The Natural History Magazine of the West* 19, no. 1 (Summer 1980): 3–9.
12. Elizabeth Hanson, *Animal Attractions: Nature on Display in American Zoos* (Princeton, NJ: Princeton University Press, 2002), 80.
13. Ibid., 74.
14. "Roosevelt African Expedition Collects for SI," *Smithsonian Institution Archives*, Retrieved March 1, 2021, https://siarchives.si.edu/collections/siris_sic_193
15. Derek Bousé, *Wildlife Films* (Philadelphia, PN: University of Pennsylvania Press, 2000), 54–6.

16. See: "USDA Animal Care Public Search Tool: List of persons licensed under the Animal Welfare Act," https://aphis-efile.force.com/PublicSearchTool/s/

17. State of Indiana v. Wildlife in Need and Wildlife in Need, Inc., Timothy Stark, Melisa Lane (Marion Superior Court 12 April 6, 2021).

18. John Berger, "Why Look at Animals?," in *About Looking* (New York: Pantheon Books, 1980), 21.

19. Brett Mizelle, "'A Man Quite as Much of a Show as His Beasts': James Capen 'Grizzly' Adams and the Making of Grizzly Bears," *Werkstattgeschichte* 56 (2010): 43.

20. Nigel Rothfels, *Savages and Beasts: The Birth of the Modern Zoo* (Baltimore, MD: Johns Hopkins University Press, 2002), 11.

21. Berger, "Why Look at Animals?" 23.

22. Randy Malamud, *An Introduction to Animals and Visual Culture* (New York: Palgrave Macmillan, 2012), 115.

23. Berger, "Why Look at Animals?" 23.

24. Malamud, *An Introduction to Animals*, 115.

25. Berger, "Why Look at Animals?" 24. His emphasis.

26. State of Indiana v. Wildlife in Need and Wildlife in Need, Inc., Timothy Stark, Melisa Lane (Marion Superior Court 12 April 6, 2021).

27. Carney Anne Nasser, "Welcome to the Jungle: How Loopholes in the Federal Endangered Species Act and Animal Welfare Act Are Feeding a Tiger Crisis in America," *Albany Government Law Review, Four Legged Clients: The Place of Animals in Our Lives and the Law* 9, no. 1 (2016): 199.

28. Xiao Xu et al., "The Genetic Basis of White Tigers," *Current Biology* 23, no. 11 (June 3, 2013): 1031–5.

29. Nicky K. Xavier, "A New Conservation Policy Needed for Reintroduction of Bengal Tiger-White," *Current Science* 99, no. 7 (October 2010): 894.

30. Xu et al., "The Genetic Basis of White Tigers."

31. Theodore H. Reed, "Enchantress! Queen of an Indian Palace, a Rare White Tigress Comes to Washington," *National Geographic* 119, no. 5 (1961): 628–41.

32. Theodore H. Reed, "Report on the National Zoological Park," *Annual Report of the Board of Regents of the Smithsonian Institution* (Washington, DC: Government Printing Office, 1961), 133.

33. Jaren Horsley, "Eleven Years of White Tigers," *Spots & Stripes* 8, no. 3 (Washington, DC: Friends of the National Zoo, 1971): 3.

34. Theodore H. Reed, "Report on the National Zoological Park," *Annual Report of the Board of Regents of the Smithsonian Institution* (Washington, DC: U.S. Government Printing Office, 1964), 112.

35. Horsley, "Eleven Years of White Tigers," 3.

36. Phil Casey, "White Tigers: A Zoo Story," *Washington Post*, August 1, 1974.

37. *Annual Report of the Board of Regents of the Smithsonian Institution*, 1964, 111.

38. After attending a performance one could (and still can) visit Siegfried & Roy's Secret Garden and Dolphin Habitat at the Mirage, a self-described "animal sanctuary," where visitors can pay to feed and touch dolphins.

39. Association of Zoos and Aquariums, *AZA Species Survival Plan® (SSP) Program Handbook* (Silver Spring, MD: Association of Zoos and Aquariums, 2021), https://assets.speakcdn.com/assets/2332/aza_species-survival-plan-program-handbook.pdf

40. "The Price of Wild Animals," *Daily Alta California* 42, no. 14204 (July 23, 1888): 2.

41. Samuel Hopkins Adams, "The Training of Lions, Tigers, and Other Great Cats from Personal Interviews with the Leading Trainers in the World," *McClure's Magazine* 15, no. 5 (September 1900): 387–98, 388.

42. Humane Society, "Dangerous Incidents Involving Bears, Big Cats and Primates in the United States 1990–Present," n.d., www.humanesociety.org/sites/default/files/docs/dangerous_incidents_bears_bigcats_primates_110119.pdf

43. Malamud, *An Introduction to Animals*, 118–19.

Bibliography

Abidin, Crystal. *Internet Celebrity: Understanding Fame Online*. Bingley: Emerald Publishing House, 2018.

Adams, Bluford. *E Pluribus Barnum: The Great Showman & The Making of U.S. Popular Culture*. Minneapolis, MN: University of Minnesota Press, 1997.

Adams, Samuel Hopkins. "The Training of Lions, Tigers, and Other Great Cats. From Personal Interviews with the Leading Trainers in the World." *McClure's Magazine* 15, no. 5 (September 1900): 387–98.

Ahmed, Sara. *The Cultural Politics of Emotion*. New York, NY: Routledge, 2004.

Alexander, Michelle. *The New Jim Crow: Mass Incarceration in the Age of Colorblindness*. New York, NY: The New Press, 2010.

Anderson, Benedict. *Imagined Communities: Reflections on the Origin and Spread of Nationalism*. New York, NY: Verso Books, 1991.

Anderst, Leah. "Calling to Witness: Complicating Autobiography and Narrative Empathy in Marlon Riggs's *Tongues Untied*." *Studies in Documentary Film* 13, no. 1 (2019): 73–89.

Annual Report of the New York Zoological Society, Vol. 7. New York, NY: New York Zoological Society, 1902.

Association of Zoos and Aquariums. *AZA Species Survival Plan® (SSP) Program Handbook*. Silver Spring, MD: Association of Zoos and Aquariums, 2021.

Auslander, Philip. "Digital Liveness: A Historico-Philosophical Perspective." *PAJ: A Journal of Performance and Art* 34, no. 3 (2012): 3–11.

Auslander, Philip. *Liveness: Performance in a Mediatized Culture*. 2nd edition. New York, NY: Routledge, 2008.

Bainbridge, Caroline. "Box-set Mind-set: Psycho-cultural Approaches to Binge Watching, Gender, and Digital Experience." *Free Associations*, no. 75 (June 2019): 65–83.

Bakhtin, Mikhail. *Rabelais and His World*. Translated by Hélène Iswolsky. Bloomington, IN: Indiana University Press, 1986.

Banet-Weiser, Sarah. *Empowered: Popular Feminism and Popular Misogyny*. Durham, NC and London: Duke University Press, 2018.

Baron, Jaimie. *Reuse, Misuse, Abuse: The Ethics of Audiovisual Appropriation in the Digital Era*. New Brunswick, NJ: Rutgers University Press, 2021.

Bennett, Joshua. *Being Property Once Myself: Blackness and the End of Man*. Cambridge: Belknap Press, 2020.

Berger, John. "Why Look at Animals?" In *About Looking*, 1–26. New York, NY: Pantheon Books, 1980.

Berlant, Lauren. *Cruel Optimism*. Durham, NC: Duke University Press, 2011.

Boisseron, Bénédicte. *Afro-Dog: Blackness and the Animal Question*. New York, NY: Columbia University Press, 2018.

Bousé, Derek. *Wildlife Films*. Philadelphia, PA: University of Pennsylvania Press, 2000.

Braverman, Irus. *Zooland: The Institution of Captivity*. Stanford, CA: Stanford University Press, 2013.

Briziarelli, Marco and Emiliana Armano, editors. *The Spectacle 2.0: Reading Debord in the Context of Digital Capitalism*. London: University of Westminster Press, 2017.

Casey, Phil. "White Tigers: A Zoo Story." *The Washington Post*, August 1, 1974.

Chris, Cynthia. *Watching Wildlife*. Minneapolis, MN: University of Minnesota Press, 2006.

Conway, William G. "Buying Time for Wild Animals with Zoos." *Zoo Biology* 30, no. 1 (2010): 1–8.

Corner, John. "Civic Visions: Forms of Documentary." In *Television: The Critical View*. 6th edition, 207–36. Edited by Horace Newcomb. Oxford: Oxford University Press, 2000.

Crowther, Barbara. "Viewing What Comes Naturally: A Feminist Approach to Television Natural History." *Women's Studies International Forum* 20, no. 2 (1997): 289–300.

De Cristofaro, Diletta. "'Every Day Is Like Sunday': Reading the Time of Lockdown Via Douglas Coupland." *b20*, May 13, 2020. www.boundary2.org/2020/05/diletta-de-cristofaro-every-day-is-like-sunday-reading-the-time-of-lockdown-via-douglas-coupland/

Dean, Jodi. "Affective Networks." *Media Tropes* 2, no. 2 (2010): 19–44.

Debord, Guy. *The Society of the Spectacle*. Translated by Donald Nicholson-Smith. Brooklyn, NY: Zone Books, 2020.

Duffy, Brooke Erin. *(Not) Getting Paid to Do What You Love*. New Haven, CT: Yale University Press, 2017.

"Eleven Years of White Tigers." *Spots & Stripes*, 8, no. 3: 2–4, 1971.

Freeman, Elizabeth. *Time Binds: Queer Temporalities, Queer Histories*. Durham, NC: Duke University Press, 2010.

Fudge, Erica. "A Left-Handed Blow: Writing the History of Animals." In *Representing Animals*, 3–18. Edited by Nigel Rothfels. Indianapolis, IN: Indiana University Press, 2002.

Gillis, Stacy. "Sin and a Tiger Skin: The Stickiness of Elinor Glyn's Three Weeks." *Women: A Cultural Review* 29, no. 2 (2018): 216–32.

Ging, Debbie and Eugenia Siapera, editors. "Special Issue on Online Misogyny." *Feminist Media Studies* 18, no. 4 (2018): 515–24.

Givens, Terri E. *Radical Empathy: Finding a Path to Bridging Racial Divides*. Bristol: Policy Press, 2021.

Griffin, Hollis. "Living Through It: Anger, Laughter, and Internet Memes in Dark Times." *International Journal of Cultural Studies* 24, no. 3 (2021): 381–97.

Grindstaff, Laura and Susan Murry. "Reality Celebrity: Branded Affect and the Emotion Economy." *Public Culture* 27, no. 1 (2015): 109–35.

Halberstam, Jack. *In a Queer Time and Place: Transgender Bodies, Subcultural Lives*. New York, NY: New York University Press, 2005.

Hall, Judith. "The U.S. Has an Empathy Deficit." *Scientific American*, September 17, 2020. www.scientificamerican.com/article/the-us-has-an-empathy-deficit/

Hallman, Bonnie and S. Mary P. Benbow, "Family Leisure, Family Photography and Zoos: Exploring the Emotional Geographies of Families." *Social & Cultural Geography* 8, no. 6 (2007): 871–88.

Hanson, Elizabeth. *Animal Attractions: Nature on Display in American Zoos*. Princeton, NJ: Princeton University Press, 2002.

Hartley, Gary. "A Beginner's Guide to Drag Terminology." *Cape Town Magazine*, n.d. www.capetownmagazine.com/arts-culture/a-beginners-guide-to-drag-terminology/104_22_19320

Hermes, Joke and Annette Hill. "Television's Undoing of Social Distance." *European Journal of Cultural Studies* 23, no. 4 (2020): 655–61.

Horeck, Tanya. "'A Film That Will Rock You to Your Core': Emotion and Affect in *Dear Zachary* and the Real Crime Documentary." *Crime Media Culture* (2014): 1–17.

Horeck, Tanya. *Justice on Demand: True Crime in the Digital Streaming Era*. Detroit, MI: Wayne State University Press, 2019.

Humane Society. "Dangerous Incidents Involving Bears, Big Cats and Primates in the United States 1990 – Present," n.d. www.humanesociety.org/sites/default/files/docs/dangerous_incidents_bears_bigcats_primates_110119.pdf

Jackson, Zakiyyah Iman. *Becoming Human: Matter and Meaning in an Anti-Black World*. New York, NY: New York University Press, 2020.

Jenner, Mareike. *Netflix & the Re-invention of Television*. Cham: Palgrave Macmillan, 2018.

Johns-Putra, Adeline. *Climate Change and the Contemporary Novel*. Cambridge: Cambridge University Press, 2019.

Jones, Miriam. "Why Do We Love to Sing Murder Ballads? Tradition, Feminism and Bluegrass." *Overland*, November 8, 2017. https://overland.org.au/2017/11/why-do-we-love-to-sing-murder-ballads-tradition-feminism-and-bluegrass/

Joy, Stuart. "Sexual Violence in Serial Form: *Breaking Bad* habits on TV." *Feminist Media Studies* 19, no. 1 (2019): 118–29.

Joyrich, Lynne. "Reality TV Trumps Politics." *The Contemporary Condition*, November 2016. http://contemporarycondition.blogspot.com/2016/11/reality-tv-trumps-politics.html

Kellner, Douglas. *Media Spectacle*. London and New York, NY: Routledge, 2003.

King, Geoff. "'Killingly Funny': Mixing Modalities in New Hollywood's Comedy-with-Violence." In *New Hollywood Violence*, 126–43. Edited by Stephen Jay Schneider. Manchester: Manchester University Press, 2004.

Kisling, Vernon N. "Zoological Gardens of the United States." In *Zoological Gardens of the United States*, 147–80. New York, NY: CRC Press, 2001.

Kafer, Alison. *Feminist, Queer, Crip*. Bloomington, IN: Indiana University Press, 2013.

Kendall, Tina. "Affect and the Ethics of Snuff in Extreme Art Cinema." In *Snuff: Real Death and Screen Media*, 257–76. Edited by Neil Jackson, Shaun Kimber, Johnny Walker, and Thomas Joseph Watson. New York, NY: Bloomsbury, 2016.

Lagerwey, Jorie and Taylor Nygaard. "*Tiger King*'s Meme-ification of White Grievance and the Normalization of Misogyny." *Forum: Tiger King. Communication, Culture and Critique* 13, no. 4 (December 2020): 560–3.

Lobato, Ramon. "Rethinking International TV Flows Research in the Age of Netflix." *Television and New Media* (2017): 1–15.

Magnusson, Bruce and Zahi Zalloua, editors. *Spectacle*. Seattle, WA: University of Washington Press, 2016.

Malamud, Randy. *An Introduction to Animals and Visual Culture*. Cham: Palgrave Macmillan, 2012.

Mann, Lucas. "How to Miss What Isn't Gone: Thoughts on Modern Nostalgias While Watching 'The Office.'" *Los Angeles Review of Books*, May 24, 2020. https://lareviewofbooks.org/article/how-to-miss-what-isnt-gone/

Marshall, Wayne. "Social Dance in the Age of (Anti-) Social Media: Fortnite, Online Video and the Jook at a Virtual Crossroads." *Journal of Popular Music Studies* 3, no. 4 (2019): 3–15.

Marwick, Alice. *Status Update: Celebrity, Publicity, and Branding in the Social Media Age*. New Haven, CT: Yale University Press, 2013.

Marwick, Alice. "You May Know Me from YouTube: (Micro-) Celebrity in Social Media." In *A Companion to Celebrity*, 333–40. Edited by P. David Marshall and Sean Redmond. Malden, MA: Wiley and Sons, 2015.

McRobbie, Angela. *Be Creative*. Cambridge: Polity Press, 2016.

Meisenhelder, Thomas. "An Essay on Time and the Phenomenology of Imprisonment." *Deviant Behavior* 6, no. 1 (1985): 39–56.

Mercer, John and Charlie Sarson. "Fifteen Seconds of Fame: Rupaul's Drag Race, Camp, and 'Memeability.'" *Celebrity Studies* (2020): 1–15.

Meyer-Dinkgräfe, Daniel. "Liveness: Phelan, Auslander, and After." *Journal of Dramatic Theory and Criticism* 29, no. 2 (2015): 69–79.

Miller, John. *Empire and the Animal Body: Violence, Identity and Ecology in Victorian Adventure Fiction*. London: Anthem Press, 2012.

Miller, John. "Rebellious Tigers, a Patriotic Elephant and an Urdu-Speaking Cockatoo: Animals in 'Mutiny' Fiction," *Journal of Victorian Culture* 17, no. 4 (2012): 480–91.

Milliken, Christie and Steve Anderson. "The Work of Popular Documentary in the Age of Alternative Facts." In *Reclaiming Popular Documentary*, 1–11. Edited by Christie Millikin and Steve Anderson. Bloomington, IN: Indiana University Press, 2021.

Mills, Brett. *The Sitcom*. Edinburgh: Edinburgh University Press, 2009.

Milner, Ryan M. *The World Made Meme: Public Conversations and Participatory Media*. Cambridge, MA: The MIT Press, 2016.

Mitman, Gregg. *Reel Nature: America's Romance with Wildlife on Film*. 2nd edition. Seattle, WA: University of Washington Press, 2012.

Mittell, Jason. "A Cultural Approach to Television Genre Theory." *Cinema Journal* 40, no. 3 (Spring 2001): 3–24.

Mittell, Jason. *Complex TV: The Poetics of Contemporary Television Storytelling.* New York, NY and London: New York University Press, 2015.

Mizelle, Brett. "'A Man Quite as Much of a Show as His Beasts': James Capen 'Grizzly' Adams and the Making of Grizzly Bears." *Werkstattgeschichte* 56 (2010): 29–45.

Moor, Robert. "American Animals." *New York Magazine*, September 3, 2019. https://nymag.com/intelligencer/2019/09/joe-exotic-and-his-american-animals.html

Moor, Robert. "Joe Exotic: Tiger King." *Wondery.* https://wondery.com/shows/joe-exotic/

Nakamura, Lisa. "Feeling Good About Feeling Bad: Virtuous Virtual Reality and the Automation of Racial Empathy." *Journal of Visual Culture* 19, no. 1 (2020): 47–64.

Nance, Susan, Albert G. Way, William Thomas Okie, Reinaldo Funes-Monzote, Gabriel N. Rosenberg, Joshua Specht, and Sandra Swart. "Roundtable: Animal History in a Time of Crisis." *Agricultural History* 94, no. 3 (Summer 2020): 444–84.

Nasser, Carney Anne. "Welcome to the Jungle: How Loopholes in the Federal Endangered Species Act and Animal Welfare Act Are Feeding a Tiger Crisis in America." *Albany Government Law Review* (Four Legged Clients: The Place of Animals in Our Lives and the Law) 9, no. 1 (2016): 195–239.

Negra, Diane and Julia Leyda, "Querying 'Karen': The Rise of the Angry White Woman." *The European Journal of Cultural Studies* 24, no. 1 (2021): 350–7.

Newcomb, Horace and Paul M. Hirsch. "Television as Cultural Forum." *Quarterly Review of Film Studies* 8 (Summer 1983): 45–55.

Newitz, Annalee and Matt Wray, editors. *White Trash: Race and Class in America.* New York, NY: Routledge, 1997.

Ngai, Sianne. *Our Aesthetic Categories: Zany, Cute, Interesting.* Cambridge, MA: Harvard University Press, 2012.

Nichols, Bill. *Introduction to Documentary.* Bloomington and Indianapolis, IN: Indiana University Press, 2001.

Nissenbaum, Asaf and Limor Shifman. "Internet Memes as Contested Cultural Capital: The Case of 4chan's/b/Board." *New Media & Society* 19, no. 4 (2017): 483–501.

Nissenbaum, Asaf and Limor Shifman. "Meme Templates as Expressive Repertoires in a Globalizing World: A Cross-Linguistic Study." *Journal of Computer-Mediated Communication* 23, no. 5 (2018): 294–310.

Nygaard, Taylor and Jorie Lagerwey. *Horrible White People: Gender, Genre and Television's Precarious Whiteness.* New York, NY: NYU Press, 2020.

Olson, James D., and Donald R. Patten. "Museum-Zoo Relations and the Arabian Oryx." *Terra: The Natural History Magazine of the West* 19, no. 1 (Summer 1980): 3–9.

Papacharissi, Zizi. *Affective Publics: Sentiment, Technology, and Politics.* Oxford: Oxford University Press, 2015.

Pfannebecker, Mareile and James A. Smith. "Tiger King, COVID-19, and the Nature of Work." *Ceasefire*, May 20, 2020. https://ceasefiremagazine.co.uk/tiger-king-covid-19-and-the-nature-of-work/

Phelan, Peggy. *Unmarked: The Politics of Performance*. New York, NY: Routledge, 1993.

Poniewozik, James. *Audience of One: Donald Trump, Television, and the Fracturing of America*. New York, NY: Liveright Publishing Corporation, 2019.

Prasad, Pavithra. "The Casual Boredom in *Tiger King*." *Communication, Culture & Critique* 13 (2020): 571–3.

Price, Mark R. Stanley and John E. Fa. "Reintroductions from Zoos: A Conservation Guiding Light or a Shooting Star?" In *Zoos in the 21st Century: Catalysts for Conservation?*, 155–77. Edited by Alexandra Zimmermann, Matthew Hatchwell, Leslie A. Dickie and Chris West. Cambridge: Cambridge University Press, 2007.

Reed, Theodore H. "Enchantress!: Queen of an Indian Palace, a Rare White Tigress Comes to Washington." *National Geographic* 119, no. 5 (1961): 628–41.

Reed, Theodore H. "Report on the National Zoological Park." *Annual Report of the Board of Regents of the Smithsonian Institution*. Washington, DC: U.S. Government Printing Office, 1961.

Reed, Theodore H. "Report on the National Zoological Park." *Annual Report of the Board of Regents of the Smithsonian Institution. Washington*, DC: U.S. Government Printing Office, 1964.

Rothfels, Nigel. *Savages and Beasts: The Birth of the Modern Zoo*. Baltimore, MD: Johns Hopkins University Press, 2002.

Selva, Donatella. "Social Television: Audience and Political Engagement." *Television & New Media* 17, no. 2 (2016): 159–73.

Seymour, Nicole. *Bad Environmentalism: Irony and Irreverence in the Ecological Age*. Minneapolis, MN: University of Minnesota Press, 2018.

Seymour, Nicole. *Strange Natures: Futurity, Empathy, and the Queer Ecological Imagination*. Urbana, IL: University of Illinois Press, 2013.

Shanker, Priyadarshani. "Star Gazing Via Documentary." *Framework: The Journal of Cinema and Media* 58, no. 1–2 (Spring/Fall 2017): 100–18.

Sharma, Sudeep. "Netflix and the Documentary Boom." In *The Netflix Effect: Technology and Entertainment in the 21st Century*, 143–54. Edited by Kevin McDonald and Daniel Smith Rowsey. New York, NY: Bloomsbury, 2016.

Shifman, Limor. *Memes in Digital Culture*. Cambridge, MA: The MIT Press, 2013.

Simon, Ron. "The Changing Definition of Reality Television." In *Thinking Outside the Box: A Contemporary Television Genre Reader*, 179–200. Edited by Gary R. Edgerton and Brain G. Rose. Lexington, KY: The University Press of Kentucky, 2008.

Sontag, Susan. "Notes on 'Camp'." *Partisan Review* 31, no. 4 (1965): 515–30.

St. Félix, Doreen. "The Crass Pleasures of 'Tiger King.'" *The New Yorker*, April 6, 2020. www.newyorker.com/magazine/2020/04/13/the-crass-pleasures-of-tiger-king

State of Indiana v. Wildlife in Need and Wildlife in Need, Inc., Timothy Stark, Melisa Lane, No. 49D12-2002-PL-006192 (Marion Superior Court 12 April 6, 2021).

Sturgeon, Noël. *Environmentalism in Popular Culture: Gender, Race, Sexuality, and the Politics of the Natural*. Tucson, AZ: University of Arizona Press, 2009.

Sundén, Jenny and Susanna Paasonen. *Who's Laughing Now? Feminist Tactics in Social Media*. Cambridge, MA: The MIT Press, 2020.

Szczygielska, Marianna. *Queer(ing) Naturecultures: The Study of Zoo Animals*, Central European University, Ph.D. dissertation, 2017. www.etd.ceu.edu/2017/szczygielska_marianna.pdf

Taylor, Derrick Bryson. "A Timeline of the Coronavirus Pandemic." *The New York Times*, March 17, 2021. www.nytimes.com/article/coronavirus-timeline.html

"Times of COVID-19." 2020. https://timesofcovid19.temporalities.no/

Turnbull, Jonathan, Adam Seale and William M. Adams. "Quarantine Encounters With Digital Animals: More-than-Human Geographies of Lockdown Life." *Journal of Environmental Media* 1, no. 1 (2020): 6.1–6.10.

van Dooren, Thom. "Pangolins and Pandemics: The Real Source of This Crisis Is Human, Not Animal." *New Matilda*, March 22, 2020. https://newmatilda.com/2020/03/22/pangolins-and-pandemics-the-real-source-of-this-crisis-is-human-not-animal/

Wadiwel, Dinesh. "The Working Day: Animals, Capital and Surplus Time." In *Animal Labour: A New Frontier of Interspecies Justice?*, 181–206. Edited by Charlotte E. Blattner, Kendra Coulter and Will Kymlicka. Oxford: Oxford University Press, 2020.

Warhol, Robyn and Susan S. Lanser. *Narrative Theory Unbound: Queer and Feminist Interventions*. Columbus, OH: Ohio State University Press, 2015.

Waugh, Thomas " 'Acting to Play Oneself: Notes on Performance in Documentary." In *Making Visible the Invisible: An Anthology of Original Essays on Film Acting*, 64–91. Edited by Carole Zucker. Metuchen, NJ: The Scarecrow Press, 1990.

Weaver, Harlan, "Pit Bull Promises: Inhuman Intimacies and Queer Kinships in an Animal Shelter." *GLQ* 21, nos. 2–3 (2015): 343–63.

Williams, Linda. "Film Bodies: Gender, Genre, and Excess." *Film Quarterly* 44, no. 4 (Summer, 1991): 2–13.

Xavier, Nicky K. "A New Conservation Policy Needed for Reintroduction of Bengal Tiger-White." *Current Science* 99, no. 7 (October 2010): 894–95.

Xu, Xiao, Gui-Xin Dong, Xue-Song Hu, Lin Miao, Xue-Li Zhang, De-Lu Zhang, Han-Dong Yang, et al. "The Genetic Basis of White Tigers." *Current Biology* 23, no. 11 (June 3, 2013): 1031–5.

Contributor Bios

Vanessa Bateman is a doctoral candidate in Art History, Theory, and Criticism at the University of California San Diego, where she is also pursuing a Graduate Specialization in Anthropogeny (the study of human origins) from the Center for Academic Research and Training in Anthropogeny (CARTA). Her research focuses on the history and representation of animals in art and visual culture from the 19th century until today.

Hannah Boast is Lecturer/Assistant Professor (Ad Astra Fellow) at University College Dublin. She was previously Leverhulme Early Career Fellow at University of Warwick. Her book *Hydrofictions: Water, Power and Politics in Israeli and Palestinian Literature* was published by Edinburgh University Press in 2020. Her work has been published in journals including *Green Letters*, *Journal of Commonwealth Literature*, and *Textual Practice*.

Kate Fortmueller is Assistant Professor at the University of Georgia. Her writing about film and television labor has appeared in journals including *Film History*, the *Historical Journal of Film, Radio, and Television*, and *Media Industries*. She is the author of *Beneath the Stars: How actors and extras helped shape the landscape of production* and *Hollywood Shutdown: Production, Distribution, and Exhibition in the Time of COVID* (both University of Texas Press, 2021).

Tanya Horeck is Associate Professor of Film, Media & Communication at Anglia Ruskin University in Cambridge, England. She has published widely on contemporary film, television, and digital media culture, with a focus on gender, affect, and violence. She is the author of the book *Public Rape: Representing Violation in Fiction and Film* and the co-editor of two anthologies, *The New Extremism in Cinema* and *Rape in Stieg Larsson's Millennium Trilogy and Beyond*. Her latest book is *Justice on Demand: True Crime in the Digital Streaming Era*.

Jorie Lagerwey is Associate Professor of Television Studies at University College Dublin. She and Taylor Nygaard are co-authors of *Horrible White People: Gender, Genre, and Television's Precarious Whiteness* (2020), an examination of gender, race, and fragility in postrecession TV comedy. She is also the author of *Postfeminist Celebrity and Motherhood: Brand Mom* (2016). Her work on gender, genre, race, and celebrity has appeared in *Cinema Journal, TV and New Media, Celebrity Studies,* Flow, and elsewhere.

Taylor Nygaard is a Faculty Associate in the Department of English's Film and Media Studies division at Arizona State University. She and Jorie Lagerwey are co-authors of *Horrible White People: Gender, Genre, and Television's Precarious Whiteness* (2020), an examination of gender, race, and fragility in postrecession TV comedy. Her work about identity, television, digital culture, and media industries has appeared in *Feminist Media Studies, TV and New Media,* Flow, and elsewhere.

Nicole Seymour is Associate Professor of English and Affiliated Faculty in Environmental Studies and Queer Studies at California State University, Fullerton. Her first book, *Strange Natures: Futurity, Empathy, and the Queer Ecological Imagination* (University of Illinois), won the 2015 Book Award from the Association for the Study of Literature and Environment. Her most recent book is *Bad Environmentalism: Irony and Irreverence in the Ecological Age* (University of Minnesota Press), which the *Chicago Review of Books* included in their list of "The Best Nature Writing of 2018."

Index